Jessica Elliott Dennison

how to
assemble
the
perfect
meal

SALAD FEASTS

Photography by Matt Russell

hardie grant books

contents

Dedicated to Philip, Rosie, Ben and Jono.
For it was your words of encouragement that
led to the making of this book.

THE
+
ART
+
OF
+
ASSEMBLING

ASSEMBLE was the word that kept coming to mind when writing this book: the idea of taking a few good ingredients and tumbling them onto a big sharing platter, without the worry of complicated techniques or hard-to-find ingredients. This is my relaxed approach to connecting over food, which I've combined with realistic guidance on how you can quickly build interesting flavours and textures in your everyday cooking.

CHAPTER 1 guides you through my trusty go-to ingredients. These are the reliable tins of beans, nutty spice blends, fragrant dressings and bright pickles that I call upon to quickly elevate everyday vegetables into brilliant meals. The recipes in CHAPTERS 2 AND 3 are all generous, flavour-packed salads; each exciting and satisfying enough to be enjoyed as a main meal in its own right. I've divided them up by cooking times and designed the quantities to feed 4, or 2 plus a packed lunch the next day. There's the fig and halloumi salad with basil oil and pistachios (page 34), a delicious supper you can get on the table in just 10 minutes. If you've got 15 minutes, try making the avocado noodles with coconut and edamame beans with a lime and ginger dressing (page 54). Then there are slightly slower, often only one- or two-pan dishes, where a few minutes of roasting time in a hot oven or griddle pan transforms everyday vegetables into stars of the show. Among others taking centre stage are the sticky roast tomatoes in orzo pasta with dukkah and thyme (page 95), ready in just 25 minutes, and the comforting pumpkin that's roasted until charred and sweet then served up with pearl barley, hazelnuts and crispy sage (page 130), which comes together in 45 minutes.

FEAST
MENUS

———

A selection of menus
pairing the flavour ideas
in Chapter 4 with complementary
salads are included at the back
of the book (pages 146—152).
They're themed on the seasons,
regionally inspired flavours and
occasions. You could either
pick out some of the elements
from a menu or rustle up the
whole feast.

In CHAPTER 4 I give ideas for adding interest to everyday classics like perfectly cooked eggs, roast chicken, vegetable fritters and simply prepared fish. For times when you want to do a bit more cooking and create a larger sharing feast, I've provided a selection of menus matching these flavour ideas to complementary salads. These are located at the back of the book (see left). Roasting a chicken in ginger, turmeric and yoghurt (page 136), for example, turns it into an ideal match for the pickled red cabbage slaw with ginger and pomegranate (page 44) and crispy onion rice with roast broccoli salad (page 117), giving you an Indian-inspired table. Or, instead, roast the chicken in harissa and coriander butter (page 137) and serve along with the baked pitta salad with cherries and almonds (page 58) or sticky pomegranate beetroot with pistachio grains (page 115) for a Middle Eastern-inspired feast.

In developing these recipes, I've tried to strike a balance between attainable and simple, and inspiring and informative. Throughout, I've considered my friends who don't work in the food industry, who might not be as confident in the kitchen or living on the doorstep of London's food markets and specialist stockists. In fact, it was those friends who kindly tested these recipes, out in rural Scotland and Australia, where the climate and food landscape differ from where I cook in my small London kitchen.

You'll notice vegetables feature heavily in the recipes. It's not that I don't enjoy meat or fish, I really do. But I find vegetables, especially when enjoyed in season, are most inspiring to eat and cook with. Plus, I'd rather treat meat and fish as a smaller element or garnish, as that way I can afford to buy the tastiest, very best quality from a supplier I trust.

My hope is for you to keep *Salad Feasts* on your kitchen counter as an everyday guide, not neatly tucked away on the shelf. I want you to bend over your favourite pages and to scribble down a note of substitute ingredients you've made. I urge you to treat the recipes as a starting point, then have a play using whatever's already in the fridge or cupboard, as it's this listening to your instincts that will enhance your cooking and make these recipes your own. More than anything, I want you to enjoy the straightforward process of tossing a few good ingredients onto a platter then placing it down on the table to share with the ones you love. Not much in life tops that feeling.

JESS

———

@FOODJESS

INGREDIENT SUBSTITUTES

Friends have told me that if they're looking at a recipe and don't have the exact ingredients listed, or are unfamiliar with the exotic-sounding oil or paste that's called for, they'll just skip making that recipe altogether.

That's why in this book, I've included substitutes – a list with each of my recipes providing alternatives that are designed to make your salad-making really flexible and easy, no matter the season or availability of shops near you. Perhaps I've used Brussels sprouts in a recipe but it's mid-summer and Brussels are nowhere to be seen; or maybe the divisive green sprouts are just not your thing. If that's the case, chop a broccoli head, some cauliflower or even a substitute cabbage instead. Use the recipe as a loose guide, get a feel for the method, standout textures and flavours then make it your own. Follow your instincts and you'll be onto something brilliant.

Likewise, substitute if there's an ingredient that's more specialist or outside your normal weekly shop. For example, you don't need to rush out and buy a big bottle of pomegranate molasses if that's what I've used; just try the splash of vinegar and honey I've suggested instead.

When suggested ingredient substitutes are not like-for-like – for example, dried sour cherries in place of fresh pear in the radicchio and Stilton recipe on page 32 – feel free to have a play and adjust quantities to your taste.

Kit for speedy cooking

I like to keep kitchen equipment pretty minimal, but there are a few things I use on a daily basis that make pulling together these recipes super-quick and easy. Investing in a really good knife and sharpener will make your cooking far more enjoyable. I find a quality speed peeler, grater, Microplane, blender and frying or griddle pan helpful too. A mandolin isn't a must but is great for finely shaving vegetables.

HOW TO ASSEMBLE A HEARTY SALAD

The wonderful thing about making a salad is that it's a relaxed, stress-free way of cooking, with endless possibilities for customisation. However, to remove the guesswork from how I've designed these recipes, I've provided this loose template.

By keeping these steps in mind and taking a look at the ingredient substitutes list, hopefully you'll have the confidence to experiment and make these recipes your own.

Pick Your Leading Vegetables

What's lingering in your fridge that needs using up? What's cheap, in season and abundant in the shops and markets at the moment?

Have a think about how you're going to treat your leading vegetable to make it that bit more special:

— Raw and shaved with a speed peeler to give it delicacy and shape?

— Roasted in a hot oven until intensely sweet and caramelised?

— Steamed or blanched, keeping it super-fresh and vibrant?

— Griddled or charred, imparting a deep, rich smokiness?

Then give a thought to your additional vegetables and herbs: how can you chop or prepare them differently? Could you tear in whole herbs so that they take on the role of a salad leaf, or perhaps finely shred them, distributing their fragrance to lift the other ingredients?

Pay attention to building contrast in colour and texture here. Consider whether a few different-coloured vegetables would make the dish look extra-inviting. If your leading vegetable is fluffy sweet potato, you could throw in some crunchy greens like sugar snap peas rather than steamed carrot, which offers a similar vibe to the potato.

A Filling Base

Next, consider what's going to be the hearty, filling bit of the meal which keeps you happy and satisfied until sitting down to eat the next one.

Whatever base you pick here will help guide which flavour direction the salad goes In. Noodles call for a hot and sour soy-based dressing, whereas a grain like couscous is better suited to rich, harissa flavours, some freshly chopped parsley and a handful of dried fruit.

+

Some Interesting Contrast

Throw in something unexpected here: a tangy quick pickle, a bitter leaf, a salty aged cheese, or a surprising pop of sweetness from a torn Medjool date. It's these original touches that keep every forkful unique.

+

Crunch & Added Texture

Some crushed seeds, a handful of croutons, a scattering of toasted nuts – these are all quick, easy ways to elevate your salad into a complete, satisfying meal. Have a play with toasting whole spices to awaken their aromas; it's a brilliant way to add instant depth and interest.

+

A Memorable Dressing to Bring It All Together

Sometimes it's just the simplest drizzle of extra-virgin olive oil, pinch of sea salt and squeeze of lemon that pulls beautiful ingredients together. At other times, a vibrant mix of chilli, fish sauce and lime juice is what's needed to elevate a dish.

The key with dressing is to taste regularly. Keep stirring, tweaking and tasting until you're happy with the balance of flavours, and then toss it through the dish and taste again. It's these small details that will transform a good meal into an exceptional one.

A
NOTE ON
SOURCING

Oils

I suggest keeping two types of oil on your kitchen counter: a subtle everyday olive or vegetable oil for cooking, and a bolder extra-virgin bottle to use for dressing. One of my favourites is Brindisa's Spanish extra-virgin olive oil; its grassy, peppery flavours make it ideal for finishing off dishes.

Dairy

I like to use free-range, medium eggs. Butter is always salted, but that's just personal preference.

Meat & Fish

As they make up such a small part of my everyday eating, I like to buy the highest-welfare, best-quality meat and fish that I can afford. MSC and RSPCA labels are helpful welfare markers when shopping in the supermarkets. I'd also recommend getting to know your local fishmonger and butcher as they'll share what's currently good value. They tend to have great chat too!

Fruit & Vegetables

This is the produce that guides my cooking throughout the seasons and keeps me connected to nature – the first sighting of ripe heritage tomatoes in summer; autumn's variety of pumpkins signifying the weeks of colder evenings and heartier eating ahead. It's been said over and over, but buying fruit and vegetables in their peak, ripe season is not only more cost-effective, but it will really enhance your cooking and allow you to keep things simple.

Sea Salt & Freshly Ground Pepper

Where I refer to seasoning, I prefer a flaky sea salt like Maldon. Black peppercorns are also freshly cracked.

It's about getting the people you care for round the table to enjoy a simple meal, making the most of an easy option like a hearty salad. And when more time is available, maybe even a couple of salads, plus something straightforward like a garlicky roast chicken with a loaf of bread, some good salty butter and a bottle of natural wine to try.

GO
-
TO
INGREDIENTS

A crumbling of waxy, toasted rye
bread, a punchy spoonful of salsa verde,
a tangy pickle and its colourful juices,
an aromatic scattering of dukkah, the
caramelised juice of a charred lemon;
these are the hard-working flavours
and textures I return to time and
time again.

In this chapter, I'll introduce
you to the staples of my kitchen; the
trusty spice blends, jars of dressing
and short-cut enhancers that lay the
foundations for an interesting salad
or larger feast. My intention is that
by familiarising yourself with these
go-to essentials, you will be able
to transform regular everyday
vegetables into the extraordinary.

BEANS + PULSES

Tinned beans and pulses are relatively cheap and, as they've already been cooked, can really speed things up. It's handy to rotate a few different varieties; my favourites include puy and green lentils, cannellini, butter and borlotti beans, plus chickpeas.

A humble tin of sweetcorn is the basis for quite a few of these recipes; try charring the kernels in this interesting slaw (page 57), on prawn ceviche tostadas (page 119), or form them into light, crisp fritters with a squeeze of fresh lime (page 141).

GRAINS + PASTA

Farro, pearl barley, spelt and brown rice are all grains that offer a filling, chewy bite in my salads. They're a great vehicle for carrying bold flavours. I tend to buy dried grains in bags, and then simmer a large batch in water with a halved lemon and some bay leaves, to keep in the fridge for the week ahead. If you're really short on time or want a sampler of the different varieties, there are some brilliant precooked pouches available.

Different noodle and pasta shapes are at the heart of some of my easiest recipes. Weeknights wouldn't be the same without soba noodles, pickled cavolo nero and sesame eggs (page 68), and it is orzo pasta that makes a simple tray of thyme-roasted tomatoes into a hearty supper (page 95).

A GOOD LOAF OF BREAD

It's my belief that if you invest in a really good loaf, then you're already halfway to a great, simple meal. Sometimes it's all you need, for mopping up tomato juices (page 122) or topping with Sicilian-style aubergines (page 112). Freeze a batch of garlic sourdough or rye croutons to keep on standby (see below) if you've got leftover bread to use up.

Rye Croutons

Taking a few moments to crumble some slices of rye bread into a hot frying pan is worth doing for the crisp and chewy, almost waxy-textured bites you end up with. They're fantastic for soaking up the horseradish and beetroot juices on page 50 and adding a nutty crunch to fresh, juicy figs, radicchio and halloumi (page 34).

3 slices (250 g/9 oz) pumpernickel rye bread

+ Crumble the rye bread into large crumbs then toast in a dry frying pan (skillet) over a medium heat for 4–5 minutes until crisp, toasted and chewy. Once cool, store in the freezer for up to 3 weeks.

Garlic Sourdough Croutons

Chewy torn bread that's lightly fried in garlic oil and sprinkled with sea salt – there's little wonder these are an instant crowd pleaser. They transform a bunch of roasted grapes into a substantial dinner (page 111) and add a delicious crunch to the pickled fennel and whipped ricotta recipe (page 92).

2 tablespoons extra-virgin olive oil
2 slices (150 g/5 oz) sourdough bread, torn into bite-size pieces
2 garlic cloves, peeled and crushed
½ teaspoon sea salt flakes

+ Heat the oil in a large frying pan (skillet) and fry the bread and garlic over a medium heat for 5–6 minutes until golden. Stir in the salt then set aside to cool and further crisp up. Once cool, store in the freezer for up to 3 weeks. (Allow them to come up to room temperature before using.)

NUTS, SEEDS + SPICES

Whether they're crushed then scattered to add some last-minute crunch, or blitzed until creamy in a bright coriander chutney (page 100), nuts and seeds are a great addition to any salad. Toasting them for a few minutes in a dry frying pan will release their natural oils, further amplifying their flavour.

Dukkah

This is my favourite blend of toasted almonds, sunflower seeds, sesame seeds and spices, inspired by the Middle East. You can buy dukkah, but making your own jar is really simple and a satisfying ritual to get in the habit of. Try scattering it over shaved squash (page 45), avocado on toast or your morning eggs.

Makes 1 jar (enough for a few of the recipes that include it)

¼ teaspoon peppercorns
1 teaspoon cumin seeds
50 g (2 oz) flaked almonds
25 g (1 oz) sunflower seeds
25 g (1 oz) sesame seeds
1 teaspoon ground coriander
¼ teaspoon smoked paprika
½ teaspoon dried oregano
1 teaspoon sea salt flakes

+ Place a large frying pan (skillet) over a medium heat. Add the peppercorns and cumin seeds for 1 minute, or until fragrant, then lightly crush in a pestle and mortar. Next, toast the almonds and sunflower seeds for 2–3 minutes until golden then add to the mortar. Toast the sesame seeds for 1–2 minutes until golden, and then stir in the coriander and paprika. Add to the mortar along with the oregano and salt. Crush the mixture then tip into a jar and keep for 3 weeks (it does keep for even longer but the spices begin to dull after 3 weeks).

TIP

—

If you don't have a pestle and mortar, just put all the toasted ingredients on a chopping board and crush with a rolling pin or the base of a jar. Play about with the blend of nuts, seeds, spices and herbs – this is just a starting point. Bear in mind when making recipes using dukkah that I've held back on the salt, as the dukkah will help to season the dish.

Cashew Satay

A spoonful of this is the perfect accompaniment to any crisp, raw vegetables. It's also an instant match for anything chargrilled, especially chicken or beef skewers marinated in soy sauce.

200 g (7 oz) cashews
15 g (½ oz) fresh ginger, peeled and roughly chopped
1 red chilli, deseeded
zest of 2 limes and juice of 1
1 garlic clove
1 tablespoon soy sauce
130 ml (4½ fl oz) coconut cream
½ tablespoon fish sauce
½ tablespoon sugar (ideally brown)

+ Toast the cashews in a large frying pan (skillet) over a high heat for 2–3 minutes until golden and you can smell the natural oils being released. Transfer to a food processor along with the rest of the ingredients and blitz. Have a taste; you may want to add more lime juice. Transfer to a small bowl, or store in the freezer for up to 1 month.

TIP

—

I like to keep a batch in the freezer so that I've got some to hand for making rice paper rolls (page 71) and Indonesian-inspired bowls (page 108) when friends join us for dinner.

Sunflower Seed Gremolata

Sounds fancy, but really this is just about chopping together some toasted sunflower seeds, lemon zest and fresh herbs to give your salad a fragrant, subtle crunch. It's delicious on griddled lettuce and soft-boiled eggs (page 48).

60 g (2 oz) sunflower seeds
1 lemon
small bunch (10 g/½ oz) mint, leaves only
small bunch (15 g/½ oz) flat-leaf parsley, leaves only

+   Toast the sunflower seeds in a frying pan (skillet) over a high heat for 2 minutes so that they release their natural oils, then set aside on the corner of your chopping board to cool. Finely zest the lemon next to the seeds. Finally, chop the herbs into the lemon zest and cooled seeds until you get a rough gremolata.

Rose Harissa

Investing in a jar of this roasted chilli and rose petal spice blend is an instant way to add a rich fragrance and smoky heat to your suppers. I've tried a few different brands but loyally return to Belazu's; it's slightly more expensive but delivers a more rounded, generous flavour. The oil at the top of the jar is also brilliant for spooning over eggs on toast in the morning. Try using the rose harissa to dress charred broccoli, flatbread and chickpeas (page 102), marinate a whole roast chicken (page 137) or transform a tray of roasted parsnips (page 132).

CITRUS

Often, the simplest and best way to dress beautiful ingredients like radicchio, Stilton and pear (page 32) is with a squeeze of lemon juice, adding only a pinch of sea salt and drizzle of extra-virgin olive oil. Roasting or charring lemon in a pan gives you a sweet, caramelised edge which mellows its tart juices. The zest is great for lifting a dish, as is some finely chopped skin from a jar of preserved lemons (page 42).

Limes bring zing to many Asian-inspired recipes like the shredded mango salad (page 107), while oranges and grapefruit deliver sunny vibes to avocado-based dishes (page 42).

Lemon and Basil Pesto

I like to keep my pesto really bright by going heavy on the lemon. Keep a jar in the fridge then toss through spring greens and orecchiette (page 51), or charred courgettes, sweetcorn and borlotti beans (page 60).

½ small garlic clove
¼–½ teaspoon sea salt flakes
large bunch of basil leaves (30 g/1 oz)
30 g (1 oz) pine nuts, toasted
75 ml (2½ fl oz) extra-virgin olive oil
zest and juice of 1 lemon
20 g (¾ oz) Parmesan, finely grated

+   Bash the garlic and ¼ teaspoon of salt into a pulp. Add most of the basil and most of the pine nuts then bash to a rough paste. Drizzle in the oil then add the lemon zest, half the juice and the Parmesan. Stir to combine then check the seasoning; you may want to add more salt or lemon juice to taste. Stir in the reserved basil and pine nuts to finish.

TIP

—

I make pesto in a pestle and mortar, but if you don't have one, just blitz until combined but still chunky in a food processor, or finally chop and crush with a knife.

Store in a jar or airtight container in the fridge and it will keep for 3–4 days.

QUICK PICKLES

Setting aside a bowl of thinly sliced fruit or veg in vinegar or lemon juice, salt and sugar features prominently in my recipes as I love how pickles have the transformative power to bring a dish alive. It's the pickled radishes cutting through the sticky pork sausage in my vermicelli noodles (page 86) that make the feast so special. Similarly, the pickled watermelon in my halloumi and sundried tomato spelt (page 66).

Red onion, cucumber, fennel, cavolo nero, radish and rhubarb all get the quick pickle treatment in these recipes, but, using the same ratio of acid to sugar and salt, you can give any fresh produce a go.

radish

cavolo nero

red onion

fennel

watermelon

CHEESE + YOGHURT

I always make sure I've got a pot of natural yoghurt and some sort of cheese in the fridge. A spoonful of yoghurt mixed with a few chopped herbs or a grating of cheese can be an instant way to boost flavour in a dish.

I tend to rotate firm, salty cheese like Parmesan, salted ricotta and feta, using them to naturally season and balance sweeter flavours in a salad. Try grating halloumi to season fresh, sweet figs and bitter radicchio leaves (page 34).

A softer cheese can also lift vegetables into main-meal status. Try burrata with tomatoes and nectarines (page 39), or fried paneer in Indian-inspired chard (page 100).

Tahini Lemon Yoghurt

The Middle Eastern nature of this sauce makes it an excellent match for cumin-roasted brassicas like Brussels sprouts (page 129) or for dipping the courgette and halloumi fritters into (page 140).

150 g (5 oz) natural yoghurt
30 g (1 oz) tahini
zest and juice of ½ lemon
pinch of sea salt flakes
½ garlic clove, crushed
olive oil (optional)

+ Mix together the yoghurt and tahini then add the lemon juice, zest, salt and garlic and stir to combine. If you'd like a thinner dressing, loosen with a splash of olive oil. Keeps at its best for 3 days in the fridge. (After that, the garlic can start to overpower the dressing.)

TIP

—

Try replacing the fresh lemon and salt with a medium preserved lemon, if you have one. Peel the skin then finely dice and stir to combine. (Discard the flesh and pips as they are overly salty and bitter.)

DRIED FRUIT

Throwing in an unexpected sweet and slightly tart pop of dried fruit is a straightforward way of making your salads taste more interesting. Sour cherries, golden sultanas and sticky Medjool dates are all favourites of mine. Cranberries work brilliantly with walnuts in the orange freekeh recipe (page 90).

FRESH HERBS

Herbs are the one thing I count on most in the kitchen, each offering its unique freshness and aroma. If you find your herbs are looking slightly sad and wilted, plunge them in a bowl of cold water and they'll soon perk up.

It's the scent of crispy rosemary that keeps me returning to the pea and farfalle recipe on page 75. And there's the mint whipped through ricotta that gives it the light taste of spring (page 92).

Salsa Verde

This is the salad dressing of my dreams; chopped herbs, garlic, capers and anchovies, brought together with golden olive oil and a heavy splash of vinegar. Try it spooned over charred prawns and cannellini beans (page 46), a tumble of ripe tomatoes (page 39) or simply with some grilled mackerel (page 139).

small bunch (15 g/½ oz) parsley, leaves only
small bunch (15 g/½ oz) basil, leaves only
small bunch (15 g/½ oz) mint, leaves only
1 garlic clove
1½ tablespoons capers
30 g (1 oz) anchovies in olive oil (drained weight)
1 teaspoon Dijon mustard
2 tablespoons white or red wine vinegar
120 ml (4 fl oz) extra-virgin olive oil

+ Finely chop the herbs, garlic, capers and anchovies together on a board then place in a small bowl. Stir in the mustard, vinegar and olive oil. Store in a jar or airtight container in the fridge for 3–4 days.

Basil Oil

If the capers and anchovies in the salsa verde are not your thing, try blitzing this up instead. It's delightful for dressing bitter leaves (page 34), and any leftovers stand in as a superb alternative to pesto.

60 ml (2 fl oz) extra-virgin olive oil
⅓ garlic clove (optional)
pinch of sea salt flakes
large bunch (30 g/1 oz) basil
juice of ½–1 lemon

+ Blitz all the ingredients in a food processor, including the basil stalks and starting with the juice of half the lemon. Once you have a pourable consistency, have a taste; you may want to add more lemon juice. Store in a jar or airtight container in the fridge for 3–4 days.

Salsa Verde (page 27)

A
-
QUICK
ASSEMBLY

10–20 MINUTES

These are my salads for
when time is short. You
can get all these recipes
on the table in less than
20 minutes, some of them in
just 10. Yet they're still
big on flavour and texture
and are a real joy to eat.

Each has been designed to
generously feed 4 people
as a main, but they will
go even further when served
with a few other salads,
or with one of the recipes
from chapter 4 to form
an even larger feast.

RADICCHIO, STILTON + PEAR

with

toasted walnuts and rye croutons

10 MINUTES

SERVES 4

This is great to make on those days between Christmas and New Year when there's still cheese, nuts and fruit lingering about and you're looking for something other than crackers. I've used strong blue Stilton, but any cheese will do.

Have a play with the fruit and nuts too; just as long as you have something sharp and sweet to contrast with the cheese and bitter leaves, you're onto a winner.

100 g (3½ oz) walnuts
1 small radicchio
2 white chicory (endive) heads
2 firm pears
juice of 1 lemon
2½ tablespoons extra-virgin olive oil
100 g (3½ oz) Stilton
1 serving rye croutons (page 19)

+ First, toast the walnuts in a large frying pan (skillet) for 2–3 minutes over a high heat to release their natural oils (be careful not to burn them). Transfer to a plate and set aside to cool.

+ Wash the radicchio and chicory under cold water then pat dry (this will freshen and crispen the leaves). Cut away the base from each head, and then pick away the individual leaves onto a large platter; tear some and leave a few smaller ones whole.

———— To assemble

Slice the pears lengthwise, creating some thick and thinner slivers (discard the core) then place over the leaves. Immediately squeeze over the lemon juice, discarding any pips (this prevents the pears from turning brown). Drizzle over the oil, crumble on the cheese then scatter with the rye croutons. Crush the walnuts then scatter over to finish. Using your hands, gently toss everything together then serve/eat immediately.

SUBSTITUTES

—

Radicchio
red chicory (endive), frisée, rocket (arugula)

Pear
dried sour cherries, Granny Smith apple, persimmon, blackberries

Walnuts
almonds, hazelnuts, pecans

FIG, RADICCHIO + HALLOUMI

with

basil oil and pistachios

10 MINUTES

SERVES 4

When you can get your hands on perfectly ripe, in-season figs, it's only right to enjoy them very simply, with a few additional ingredients on the plate working to highlight their magnificence.

Grating over naturally salty halloumi contrasts with the figs' sweet juices, while the toasted pistachios and leaves bring some fresh crunch. A spoonful of the ridiculously easy basil oil brings the whole plate alive. This really is no-fuss, simple, seasonal eating.

60 g (2 oz) shelled pistachios
100 g (3½ oz) red butterhead lettuce
100 g (3½ oz) radicchio
1 serving basil oil (page 27)
8 ripe figs
170 g (6 oz) halloumi
4 slices (300 g/10½ oz) sourdough or rye bread

+ First, toast the pistachios in a dry frying pan (skillet) over a high heat for 1–2 minutes to release their natural oils. Transfer to the corner of your chopping board then, once cool, roughly chop.

+ Next, wash the lettuce and radicchio in a basin of cold water (this will freshen and crispen the leaves), pat dry then tear into a large mixing bowl. Pour half the basil oil over the leaves then, using your hands, gently toss to evenly coat. Transfer to a platter.

———— To assemble

Roughly tear the figs over the leaves, and then, using the large side of a box grater, grate over the halloumi. Scatter over the toasted chopped pistachios then drizzle over the remaining basil oil to finish. Serve immediately, using the bread to mop up the fantastic herby oil and fig juices.

SUBSTITUTES

—

Pistachios
hazelnuts, walnuts, pecans, almonds

Red butterhead lettuce
frisée, oak leaf lettuce,
cos (romaine) lettuce

Radicchio
chicory (endive)

TOP RIGHT: Peas, Broccolini + Butter Beans (page 38)
BOTTOM LEFT: Tomato, Nectarine + Burrata (page 39)

PEAS, BROCCOLINI + BUTTER BEANS

with

herby yoghurt and Parmesan

15 MINUTES

SERVES 4

SUBSTITUTES

—

Broccoli
asparagus

Peas
podded and skinned
broad (fava) beans

Basil/dill/mint
tarragon, chervil, parsley

As most households have a trusty bag of peas sitting in their freezer, I wanted to create an effortless recipe that celebrates them. Here, peas are included whole, but they also form the base of this delightfully silky herb and yoghurt dressing. Often I'll make a double batch of dressing then toss the extra through a bowl of pasta for a speedy meal the next day. Basil, dill and mint is my favourite herb combination with the peas, but any large handful of a soft green herb would work well.

Oh, and if you're looking for lunchbox ideas, this is a really good one for making ahead. (See photo on previous page.)

350 g (12 oz) tender-stem or purple sprouting broccoli (broccolini)
300 g (10½ oz) frozen peas
100 g (3½ oz) pine nuts
2 x 400 g (14 oz) tins butter (lima) beans in water, rinsed and drained
2½ tablespoons capers, roughly chopped
20 g (¾ oz) Parmesan

For the dressing:
125 g (4 oz) natural yoghurt
½ small garlic clove
small bunch (15 g/½ oz) basil
small bunch (15 g/½ oz) dill
small bunch (15 g/½ oz) mint, leaves only
1½ tablespoons extra-virgin olive oil
¼ teaspoon sea salt flakes
zest and juice of ½–1 lemon

+ First, bring a medium pan of water to the boil. Trim the ends off the broccoli then blanch for 3 minutes over a high heat until vibrant green. Remove with a slotted spoon, rinse under cold water then drain in a colander and set aside. Add the peas to the boiling water and cook for 1–2 minutes, rinse under cold water and drain completely.

+ Next, toast the pine nuts in a dry frying pan (skillet) over a high heat for 2–3 minutes until lightly golden and releasing their natural oils. (Pine nuts can burn easily, so stir frequently and keep an eye on them.) Transfer to a plate and set aside to cool.

——— To assemble

Blitz half the peas with the yoghurt, garlic, herbs, oil, salt and zest and juice of half the lemon in a food processor. Have a taste – you may want to squeeze in the other lemon half – then transfer to a large mixing bowl. Toss in the butter beans, remaining peas, pine nuts, capers and broccoli. Finely grate over the Parmesan to finish.

TOMATO, NECTARINE + BURRATA

with

salsa verde and toasted sourdough

15 MINUTES

SERVES 4

When it comes to summer eating, I really believe that simple is best, particularly when tomatoes are involved. Tossing the tomatoes in a little salt, oil and vinegar will draw out their natural sweetness, releasing more fragrant juices for you to mop up with burrata and bread. If you've never had it before, burrata is like an even softer buffalo mozzarella with extra cream – dreamy with a few spoonfuls of punchy salsa verde.

Remember to use ripe tomatoes at room temperature for this, not unripe and cold from the fridge. It'll take you closer to the feeling of being on holiday. And if you don't have salsa verde, or the time to make some, a few basil leaves and an extra splash of vinegar will work brilliantly too. (See photo on previous page.)

550 g (1 lb 3 oz) ripe tomatoes, at room temperature
    (a variety of colours is nice)
2 teaspoons red wine vinegar
2 teaspoons extra-virgin olive oil
½ teaspoon sea salt flakes
1 teaspoon sugar (ideally white)
2 ripe nectarines, at room temperature
4 slices (300 g/10½ oz) sourdough bread
2 medium balls (350 g/12 oz) burrata
1 serving salsa verde (page 27)

+   First, roughly chop the tomatoes – aim for big, random shapes that will hold the salsa verde, not uniform dice. Put them in a medium bowl along with the vinegar, oil, salt and sugar. Halve the nectarines, discard the stones then roughly tear large chunks into the tomato mixture. Gently toss then set aside to quickly marinate.

+   Toast or griddle the bread.

——— To assemble

Spoon the tomato mixture on to a large serving platter, including all the marinade juices. Tear over the burrata then drizzle over the salsa verde to finish. Serve immediately with the bread.

SUBSTITUTES

—

Nectarines
peaches, apricots, strawberries

Red wine vinegar
white wine vinegar, malt vinegar, cider vinegar

Burrata
buffalo mozzarella, feta

A Quick Assembly (10–20 Minutes)

BLOOD ORANGE, LENTIL + FENNEL

with

Manchego and hazelnuts

15 MINUTES

SERVES 4

SUBSTITUTES

—

Green lentils
puy lentils, cannellini beans,
farro, buckwheat

Blood orange
regular orange, ruby grapefruit
(reduce the amount of lemon if
using grapefruit as they are
slightly more acidic)

Manchego
Parmesan, pecorino, firm salted ricotta

TIP

—

Don't worry if your hazelnuts aren't
blanched. Just rub the nuts between
some sheets of kitchen paper when
they come out of the oven. This will
wipe away most of the papery skins.

Blood oranges bring a very welcome injection of colour into grey, winter lunchtimes in Britain. I love peeling them open to discover whether they're purple and sweet all the way through, or slightly more acidic with a few light-pink blushes. They only have a short season, so throughout the rest of the year I use regular oranges or grapefruit to make this salad.

Tinned green lentils provide an easy, filling base for the sliced oranges, with shaved fennel delivering an aniseed note and the roasted hazelnuts some crunch. I use a few shavings of Manchego to naturally season the mixture, but you could use any hard, salty cheese that's in your fridge. Be sure to hold onto the juice that's released from the oranges as you prepare them on your chopping board; it's fantastic for dressing the peppery rocket.

80 g (3 oz) blanched hazelnuts (see tip)
1 large fennel bulb (ideally with a few fronds still intact)
2 blood oranges
2 x 390 g (13¾ oz) tins green lentils in water, rinsed and drained
small bunch (15 g/½ oz) dill, leaves only, picked
3 tablespoons extra-virgin olive oil
1–2 lemons
½–1 teaspoon sea salt flakes
100 g (3½ oz) wild rocket (arugula)
65 g (2¼ oz) Manchego
4 slices (300 g/10½ oz) sourdough bread (optional)

+ First, preheat the oven to 200°C (400°F/Gas 6). As the oven heats up, roast the hazelnuts in a single layer on a baking tray for 8–9 minutes until golden and fragrant. Transfer to a plate and set aside to cool. Wash the fennel under cold water, pat dry then slice lengthwise, as finely as you can (if you have one, a mandolin is handy for achieving really thin slices). Discard the white inner core and reserve any leafy fronds for garnish, and then transfer to a large mixing bowl.

+ Next, slice the top and bottom off the oranges and then carefully cut away the peel and white pith. Cut the flesh into horizontal slices then add to the fennel, along with any juice remaining on your chopping board. Ensure the lentils are fully drained then add to the bowl with the dill leaves. Drizzle in the oil, squeeze in the juice of 1 lemon (discarding any pips) and add ½ teaspoon of salt.

+ Using your hands, gently toss the salad, ensuring it's evenly coated. Check the seasoning; depending on the acidity of your oranges, you may want to add more lemon juice or salt (bear in mind that the Manchego will add saltiness too).

——— To assemble

Wash the rocket in a basin of cold water (this will freshen and crispen the leaves), pat dry then toss through the lentil and orange mixture and transfer to a large platter. Roughly crush or chop the cooled hazelnuts then scatter over, along with any reserved fennel fronds. Using a speed peeler or grater, shave over the Manchego to finish. Serve/eat immediately, with the bread to mop up those lovely citrussy juices, if using.

HOT SMOKED SALMON, AVOCADO + GRAPEFRUIT

with

toasted sunflower seeds and pickled radishes

15 MINUTES

SERVES 4

SUBSTITUTES

—

Hot smoked salmon
hot smoked trout, smoked mackerel, tinned tuna, cooked prawns (shrimps)

Grapefruit
blood orange, orange

Preserved lemon
finely grated lemon or grapefruit zest

Rocket
watercress, frisée, baby spinach

It must have been while working in Australia that I picked up the inspiration for this dish. It's exactly the kind of thing that would be served in the bright, airy cafes for which the country has become so renowned. The grapefruit and pickles cut nicely through the rich avocado and oily fish, and I love the subtle but surprising crunch you get from the toasted fennel seeds.

If you have any good bread to hand, this would also make a happy tray of open sandwiches. Replacing the hot smoked salmon with the trout or mackerel from chapter 4 (pages 138 and 139) would also be lovely too.

1 small red onion, finely sliced
100 g (3½ oz) radishes, finely sliced
juice of 1 lemon
¼ teaspoon sea salt flakes
2 teaspoons fennel seeds
55 g (2 oz) sunflower seeds
120 g (4 oz) rocket (arugula)
small bunch (20 g/¾ oz) flat-leaf parsley, leaves only
2 preserved lemons (optional)
250 g (9 oz) hot smoked salmon
2 ripe avocados, halved and stones removed
2 ruby grapefruits
2½ tablespoons extra-virgin olive oil

+ Place the onion and radishes in a small bowl. Squeeze over the lemon juice, discarding any pips, then stir in the salt and set aside to lightly pickle.

+ Meanwhile, toast the fennel and sunflower seeds in a frying pan (skillet) over a high heat for 2–3 minutes to release their natural oils. Transfer to a plate to cool.

+ Wash the rocket in a basin of cold water (this will freshen and crispen the leaves), pat dry then place in a large mixing bowl.

+ Roughly chop the parsley leaves. Cut the skin off the preserved lemons and finely slice, if using (discard the flesh as it's salty and bitter). Flake the salmon and slice the avocados. Cut off the top and bottom of the grapefruits, and then carefully slice away the peel and white pith. Slice into segments.

———— To assemble

Add the parsley, preserved lemons, salmon, avocados and grapefruit to the rocket along with the pickled onion and radishes, including the pickling juice and any grapefruit juice on your chopping board. Drizzle over the oil then, using your hands, gently toss to combine, ensuring the salad is evenly dressed. Crush or roughly chop the cooled sunflower and fennel seeds then scatter over to finish. Serve/eat immediately.

PICKLED RED CABBAGE, GINGER + POMEGRANATE SLAW

with

cumin, lime and coriander

15 MINUTES

SERVES 4

I give red cabbage a bit of an India-meets-Persia treatment in this vibrant slaw. Sitting the cabbage in lime juice flavours and softens it slightly, making it way more pleasurable to eat than raw cabbage. To remove the seeds from the pomegranate, I'd normally just halve it then whack them out with a spoon. You can buy prepacked pomegranate seeds in most supermarkets these days too, so that makes things even easier.

On weekdays I'll eat this on its own for a light lunch, but if you want to make it more substantial, wrap it in naan bread along with some fried paneer – it is just fantastic. At weekends we'll make this for friends with my ginger, turmeric and yoghurt roast chicken on page 136.

200 g (7 oz) red cabbage, finely shredded
¼ teaspoon sea salt flakes
juice of 1 lime
60 g (2 oz) cashews
½ teaspoon ground cumin
15 g (½ oz) fresh ginger, peeled
large bunch (30 g/1 oz) coriander (cilantro), leaves only
3 tablespoons mayonnaise
200 g (7 oz) sweetheart cabbage
1 small pomegranate or 125 g (4 oz) preprepared seeds

+ Place the red cabbage in a large bowl along with the salt. Squeeze in the lime juice, give it a good stir, then set aside to lightly pickle.

+ Next, toast the cashews in a frying pan (skillet) over a high heat for 2–3 minutes until golden and you can smell the natural oils being released (be careful not to get distracted at this point as nuts can burn easily). Set aside on your chopping board to cool.

+ Toast the cumin for 1 minute (this helps to awaken the flavour) then transfer to a large mixing bowl. Finely grate the ginger then squeeze it to release the juice over the cumin (discard the grated root). Finely shred the coriander and stir into the cumin along with the mayonnaise.

+ Wash the sweetheart cabbage under cold water, pat dry then remove any tired-looking outer leaves. Finely shred, discarding the tough core at the base, then toss through the bowl of dressing.

——— To assemble

Cut open the pomegranate, pop out the seeds (discard the bitter white pith) then add to the dressed sweetheart cabbage. Add the pickled red cabbage (along with its lime marinade) then stir to combine. Roughly crush the cashews then scatter over to finish.

SUBSTITUTES

—

Sweetheart cabbage
white cabbage, savoy cabbage

Pomegranate seeds
sultanas, sour cherries, tamarind paste

Cashews
almonds, coconut flakes

SHAVED SQUASH, CHICKPEAS + SOUR CHERRIES

with

strained yoghurt and dukkah

15 MINUTES

SERVES 4

SUBSTITUTES

—

Greek yoghurt
feta (whipped in a food processor
until smooth), goat's curd

Sour cherries
raisins, sultanas, dried apricots,
dried cranberries, Medjool dates

Chickpeas (garbanzo beans)
butter (lima) beans, cannellini beans

Dukkah
roasted hazelnuts with some
toasted cumin seeds

I ask you to hear me out on the raw squash element of this dish. When you shave it really thinly with a speed peeler then toss it in lemon juice, it becomes delicate and sweet.

Thick, strained yoghurt (or labne if you can get it) is a smooth, creamy contrast to the zingy squash, with cherries bringing a pop of extra tart-sweetness. The chickpeas deliver substance and the harissa some smoky heat. Scattered with dukkah (the jar of toasted spice and nut blend that I regularly reach for), this is a seriously bold and surprising way to enjoy autumn's variety of squashes.

½ small squash (100 g/3½ oz) (coquina or butternut varieties work well)
1½ tablespoons extra-virgin olive oil
zest and juice of 1 lemon
pinch of sea salt flakes
250 g (9 oz) full-fat strained Greek yoghurt (Fage brand is great)
small bunch (15 g/½ oz) flat-leaf parsley, leaves only
400 g (14 oz) tin chickpeas (garbanzo beans) in water, rinsed and drained
50 g (2 oz) dried sour cherries, roughly chopped
½ tablespoon harissa paste (Belazu rose harissa is great)
3½ tablespoons dukkah (page 20)

+ First, using a speed peeler, remove and discard the squash skin. Continue peeling to create really thin strips of squash then place them in a large mixing bowl along with the oil. Squeeze in the lemon juice and mix thoroughly, and then leave to marinate for 5 minutes.

+ Meanwhile, in a small bowl, mix the lemon zest, salt and yoghurt until just combined. (Discard any liquid from the top of the yoghurt carton and try not to overmix as you want the yoghurt to stay nice and thick.)

+ Roughly chop the parsley leaves and add to the squash along with the chickpeas, cherries and harissa then, using your hands, gently toss, ensuring the squash is evenly coated.

———— To assemble

Smear the yoghurt onto a large platter using the back of a spoon, tumble on the dressed squash then scatter over the dukkah to finish.

CHARRED PRAWNS, CANNELLINI BEANS + FENNEL

with

salsa verde
and sourdough

15 MINUTES
SERVES 4

This is the kind of meal that's ideal for those sunny evenings when you just want to cook something quick but delicious, grab a glass of chilled wine and enjoy eating in the garden with company. I've dressed the prawns and beans in salsa verde, but basil oil, another of my quick go-to ingredients, would also be fantastic (page 27).

To give the prawns the best, juiciest, charred flavour, I always cook them quickly in a smoking-hot pan. So if you are outside, throwing them on the barbecue would be nice too.

1 tablespoon olive oil
325 g (11½ oz) unpeeled raw tiger prawns (shrimps)
150 g (5 oz) wild rocket (arugula)
1 large fennel bulb (ideally with a few fronds still intact)
400 g (14 oz) tin cannellini beans in water, rinsed and drained
1 serving salsa verde (page 27)
4 slices (300 g/10½ oz) sourdough bread

+ First, heat a large frying pan (skillet) over a high heat for 2–3 minutes until smoking. Rub the oil over the prawns and cook for 4–5 minutes in a single layer until pink and gaining a nice charred colour. (Turn the prawns halfway through cooking and cook in two batches if they don't all fit in your pan in a single layer). Set aside on a plate.

+ Next, wash the rocket in a basin of cold water (this will freshen and crispen the leaves), pat dry then set aside. Slice the fennel lengthwise as thinly as you can (discard the core and reserve any leafy fronds). A mandolin is handy for achieving really thin slices.

———— To assemble

Scatter the rocket, beans and fennel over a large platter, spoon over 2½ tablespoons of salsa verde then gently, using your hands, toss to lightly coat. Scatter over the prawns and reserved fennel fronds then place the remaining salsa verde in a nice dish for people to help themselves to. Take the bread, lots of napkins and some side plates for peeling the prawns to the table.

SUBSTITUTES

—

King prawns
calamari, crayfish in shells,
scallops in shells

Cannellini beans
butter (lima) beans, chickpeas
(garbanzo beans), green lentils

Rocket
watercress, lamb's lettuce, frisée

TIP

—

If you want to devein the prawns, cut along the back with a sharp pair of scissors then lift out and discard the black vein with the tip of a knife.

GRIDDLED LETTUCE, SOFT-BOILED EGGS + ANCHOVIES

with

sunflower seeds and Parmesan

15 MINUTES

SERVES 4

SUBSTITUTES

—

Gem lettuce
chicory (endive),
cos (romaine) lettuce,
asparagus

Sunflower seeds
hazelnuts, pine nuts,
flaked almonds

This is a bolder version of the classic Caesar and just as good. I griddle the lettuce then go heavy on the anchovies and mustard to cut through the rich soft-boiled egg yolks. If you have a ripe tomato to hand, it's worth doing the step I picked up in Madrid – rubbing its juices and seeds into the hot sourdough toast. The tomato toast gives a fragrance and sweetness that nicely balances the whole meal.

4 eggs
8 baby gem or 4 large gem lettuces
3 tablespoons olive oil
60 g (2 oz) sunflower seeds
4 slices (300 g/10½ oz) sourdough bread
1 large ripe tomato, halved (optional)
1 lemon
small bunch (15 g/½ oz) flat-leaf parsley, leaves only
2 teaspoons Dijon mustard
8 tinned anchovies in oil
25 g (1 oz) Parmesan

+ First, bring a small pan of water to the boil. Carefully add the eggs and simmer for 6 minutes on a medium heat (this time is for cooked whites and oozy yolks; simmer for 8–9 minutes if you prefer hard-boiled eggs). Remove from the pan then drop into a bowl of very cold water, cracking the base of each egg slightly (this will make peeling them easier).

+ Meanwhile, heat a large frying pan (skillet) or griddle pan until smoking. Halve the baby gems lengthwise; or if you're using large gem lettuces, cut into quarters. Drizzle 1 tablespoon of the oil over the cut sides of the lettuce and char for 2 minutes each side until blackened at the edges. Set aside, cut side up, on a large platter. Carefully wipe away any remaining oil with kitchen paper.

+ Next, reduce the heat to low and toast the seeds for 2 minutes until fragrant and beginning to turn golden. Then transfer to the corner of your chopping board to cool. Toast the bread under a grill (broiler) or in a toaster until golden. If using the tomato, rub the juice and seeds into the toasts.

+ Zest the lemon onto the chopping board and chop into the parsley leaves and cooled seeds until you get a rough gremolata. Stir together the Dijon, remaining oil and juice of half the lemon (discard any pips) in a small bowl or jug. Cut the remaining lemon half into quarter wedges. Carefully peel the eggs and pat dry.

——— To assemble

Lay the anchovies – minus most of their oil – over the lettuce. Drizzle over the mustard dressing then scatter over the gremolata. Place the eggs on top, cut them open to expose the yolk, then finely grate over the Parmesan. Serve with the lemon wedges and tomato toasts for dunking into the yolk. Eat immediately.

BASHED GINGER, KALE + SPROUTING PULSES

with

tamarind dressing and fried paneer

15 MINUTES

SERVES 4

I'm told they're very good for you, but it's the crunch that sprouting pulses bring to this hot and sour mix of crushed ginger, radish and kale that I like most. It's ridiculously tasty with pan-fried paneer and fresh coriander. If you can't get hold of them, a handful of beansprouts or Bombay mix makes a good stand-in for the pulses.

Throw this mixture over some poppadoms or a naan bread if you're mega-hungry. And if you don't have tamarind paste to hand, just squeeze in some lime juice instead.

2 garlic cloves
25 g (1 oz) fresh ginger, peeled
½ red onion, finely sliced
1 small red chilli
150 g (5 oz) radishes, roughly chopped
200 g (7 oz) sprouting pulses
75 g (2½ oz) kale
small bunch (20 g/¾ oz) coriander (cilantro)
3 teaspoons tamarind paste
1 teaspoon honey
¼ teaspoon sea salt flakes
1½ tablespoons vegetable oil
220 g (7½ oz) paneer, cut into 1.5 cm (½ in) cubes
½ teaspoon ground turmeric (optional)

+ First, peel the garlic and place in a pestle and mortar. Grate in the ginger (discard the tough inner root). Add the onion along with the chilli (remove the seeds if you don't like things too spicy) and bash with the pestle until you get a rough paste. Transfer to a large mixing bowl. Bash and roughly crush the radishes in the pestle and mortar. Add to the bowl along with the sprouting pulses.

+ Next, wash the kale and coriander under cold water, pat dry then finely shred (discard the tough inner kale stems and coriander stems). Add to the mixing bowl.

+ Stir the tamarind paste, honey, salt and 2 teaspoons of water together in the mortar until combined. Scrape into the large bowl along with any chilli and garlic residue.

+ Put the oil in a medium frying pan (skillet) over a high heat and fry the paneer for 2–3 minutes, or until golden and crispy at the edges. If using the turmeric, scatter over while frying; this will give your paneer an amazing yellow colour.

——— To assemble

Using your hands, toss the tamarind dressing though the kale mixture, ensuring everything is evenly coated. Scatter over the fried paneer and serve/eat immediately.

SUBSTITUTES

—

Tamarind paste
lime juice

Sprouting pulses
beansprouts, Bombay mix

Kale
spinach, cavolo nero, chard

Radishes
cucumber, deseeded ripe tomatoes

TIP

—

Don't worry if you don't have a pestle and mortar; just crush and bash everything with the side of your knife on a large, steady chopping board.

HORSERADISH BEETROOT, DILL PICKLES + RYE CROUTONS

with

savoy cabbage, capers and dill

15 MINUTES

SERVES 4

SUBSTITUTES

—

Horseradish
Dijon mustard

Savoy cabbage
sweetheart, white or red cabbage

Mayonnaise
natural yoghurt

Without a doubt, the inspiration for this meal comes from a weekend trip to Copenhagen. After a morning of cycling round the city, we stopped at a cafe for an open rye sandwich. Mine was topped with beetroot, horseradish and house pickles; the kind of flavours I toss through shredded savoy cabbage here.

Rather than serving the veggies on a slice of bread, I like to toast the rye into chewy, waxy crumbs – one of my standby go-to ingredients (page 19).

This mixture is a substantial delight as it is, but bring it together with some pickled herring, smoked mackerel or boiled eggs (page 144) and potato salad (page 103) and you've got a larger Scandi-style feast.

3 tablespoons mayonnaise
2½ teaspoons creamed horseradish
1 tablespoon honey
juice of ½–1 lemon
2 tablespoons capers, drained and finely chopped
5 dill pickles, drained and finely chopped
300 g (10½ oz) savoy cabbage
600 g (1 lb 5 oz) precooked beetroots (beets), at room temperature
1 serving rye croutons (page 19).
small bunch (15 g/½ oz) dill, leaves only

+ First, combine the mayonnaise, horseradish and honey in a large mixing bowl. Add the juice of half the lemon, the capers and pickles. Stir and have a taste; you may want to add more lemon juice.

+ Finely shred the cabbage (discard the tough outer leaves and inner core), then, using your hands, scrunch into the mayonnaise mixture. Set aside for 5 minutes to marinate and soften.

———— To assemble

Drain and roughly chop the beetroots then add to the cabbage along with the rye croutons. Transfer to a large platter then scatter over the dill leaves to finish.

SPRING
GREEN
ORECCHIETTE

with

lemon pesto and peas

This is simplicity at its best – good pasta, some homemade citrussy pesto and a large handful of greens and peas. I use orecchiette pasta as it's one of my favourites, and I love how individual peas sit neatly in the little 'ears'. It's not sold absolutely everywhere, so when I do come across it, I'll stock up on a few bags. Try your local Italian deli for some, or take a look at the substitutes; you can easily switch to whichever pasta's sitting in your cupboard.

A tub of this light pasta salad travels particularly well, so I'll often pack it for road trips and picnics.

15 MINUTES

SERVES 4

350 g (12 oz) orecchiette
150 g (5 oz) frozen peas
45 g (1½ oz) pine nuts
300 g (10½ oz) spring greens
1 serving lemon and basil pesto (page 23)

+ First, bring a large pan of water to the boil, and then add the orecchiette and cook for the time stated on the packet (around 8–9 minutes for al dente). Add the peas for the last minute of cooking time. Refresh under plenty of cold water then drain completely and place in a large mixing bowl.

+ Meanwhile, toast the pine nuts in a large frying pan (skillet) over a high heat for 2–3 minutes until lightly golden and releasing their natural oils. (Pine nuts can burn easily, so stir frequently and keep an eye on them.) Transfer to a small plate and allow to cool.

+ Wash the spring greens, pat dry then finely shred (discard the tough inner core). Put the frying pan back on a high heat then add the greens along with a few splashes of water. Blanch for 1 minute until vibrant green and the water has evaporated.

———— To assemble

Toss together the pesto, spring greens, pasta and peas then transfer to a large platter and serve.

SUBSTITUTES

—

Orecchiette
farfalle, conchiglie, penne

Spring greens
spinach, Swiss chard,
rocket (arugula), asparagus

Avocado + Coconut Noodles (page 54)

AVOCADO + COCONUT NOODLES

with

edamame beans, lime and ginger

15 MINUTES

SERVES 4

When I'm home late from a long day's cooking but still craving something flavour-packed and comforting to round off the day, this is what I make. These are ingredients I tend always to have in my kitchen, but you could easily mix it up with whatever veggies are in your fridge, some shredded chicken or the Chilli Fried Eggs on page 144.

I haven't included it as an essential, but half a teaspoon of wasabi paste in place of the ginger works really well too. And as the noodles are chilled, they'll happily sit in the dressing, making this a good option for packing into tomorrow's lunchbox. (See photo on previous page.)

200 g (7 oz) egg noodles
250 g (9 oz) frozen podded edamame beans
60 g (2 oz) sunflower seeds
100 g (3½ oz) desiccated (unsweetened shredded) coconut
1–2 teaspoons chilli flakes
60 ml (2 fl oz) soy sauce
2 tablespoons honey
juice of 2 limes
20 g (¾ oz) fresh ginger, peeled and finely grated
6 spring onions (scallions)
2 ripe avocados, halved and stones removed

+ First, bring a large pan of water to the boil then cook the noodles over a high heat for the time stated on the packet (around 5 minutes). Add the beans to the pan for the last 30 seconds of cooking then refresh the noodles and beans under plenty of cold water, drain in a colander and set aside.

+ Meanwhile, toast the sunflower seeds for 2 minutes in a frying pan (skillet) over a high heat so that they release their natural oils. Add the coconut to the pan for 30 seconds to lightly toast then transfer the seeds and coconut to a plate to cool.

+ In a large bowl mix together 1 teaspoon chilli flakes, the soy sauce and honey. Squeeze in the lime juice and add the ginger, then stir to combine. Shred the spring onions by cutting them finely on an angle, discarding any tough green upper layers, and slice the avocados. Add to the bowl.

———— To assemble

Gently toss the cold drained noodles, beans, seeds and coconut in the soy sauce and avocado mixture. Have a taste – you may want to add more chilli flakes – then serve.

SUBSTITUTES

—

Egg noodles
soba noodles, rice noodles

Desiccated (unsweetened shredded) coconut
shaved fresh coconut, coconut chips

Sunflower seeds
pumpkin seeds

Lime
rice wine vinegar

SMOKY TOMATO + FETA BEANS

with

avocado, coriander and toasted pumpkin seeds

20 MINUTES

SERVES 4

Okay, so here I am asking you to place tomatoes directly over the flame of your gas hob, but please don't be alarmed. Use a pair of tongs, keep your eye on things and you'll be rewarded with a charred flavour that intensifies the tomato's natural sweetness. If your stove isn't gas or you're still not convinced about cooking directly over flames, placing the tomatoes, chilli and garlic in a very hot pan will give a similar vibe.

If you're among a very hungry crowd, serve this up at the table with some warm tortillas alongside, and then everyone can build their own amazing burrito-style wraps.

500 g (1 lb 2 oz) ripe tomatoes, at room temperature
1 red chilli
2 garlic cloves
¼ teaspoon sea salt flakes, plus a pinch
50 g (2 oz) pumpkin seeds
2 x 400 g (14 oz) tins black-eyed beans in water, rinsed and drained
2 tablespoons olive oil
½ teaspoon ground cumin
2 limes
2 ripe avocados, halved and stones removed
small bunch (20 g/¾ oz) coriander (cilantro)
½ cucumber, deseeded and finely diced
200 g (7 oz) feta
4 tortilla wraps (optional)

SUBSTITUTES

—

Pumpkin seeds
sunflower seeds, flaked almonds

Black-eyed beans
kidney, cannellini, butter (lima) beans

Feta
salted ricotta, mature cheddar

+   First, pierce a few small slashes into half the tomatoes, the chilli and garlic. If using a gas stove, put a flame on high and, using tongs, place the pierced tomatoes and chilli directly on the flame for around 5 minutes until charred and blistered. (Light two flames if one isn't big enough to cook everything at once.) Peel the garlic then place in the flame for 30 seconds. (You can do all the above in a very hot griddle pan if using an induction stove.)

+   Place the charred tomatoes, chilli and garlic in a food processor along with a pinch of salt. Blitz until smooth then transfer to a large mixing bowl.

+   Next, toast the pumpkin seeds in a large frying pan (skillet) over a high heat for 2 minutes or until beginning to pop then transfer to a plate to cool. Roughly chop the remaining tomatoes and add to the pan along with the beans, olive oil and cumin. Cook over a high heat for 5–6 minutes until blistered and popped then place in the bowl of dressing. Squeeze in the juice of 1 lime and add the salt then toss. Transfer to a large platter.

+   Chop the avocado flesh into small dice. Pick the coriander leaves and finely slice the stalks. Cut the remaining lime into wedges.

——————— To assemble

Scatter the avocado, cucumber and coriander over the beans along with the cooled pumpkin seeds. Crumble over the feta and serve with the lime wedges. Eat as is or, if you're really hungry, stuff into a tortilla.

SWEET PEPPER + ARTICHOKE FARRO

with

basil and feta

When we first lived in Edinburgh, Friday night was all about sourdough pizza at Söderberg, an excellent Scandinavian bakery. I'd always order their veggie option, generously topped with artichokes, peppers and feta, but sadly it's no longer on their menu. So here's my version, without going to the effort of fermenting and proving your own sourdough.

All the hard work on the flavour front is delivered by the jarred antipasti, so try to buy decent quality. Slice the peppers as finely as you can; you'll get an incredible sweetness that contrasts beautifully with the salty feta.

20 MINUTES
SERVES 4

2 lemons, halved
230 g (8 oz) quick-cook farro
2 bay leaves (optional)
2 orange or yellow (bell) peppers (green peppers don't work here)
140 g (5 oz) jarred sundried tomatoes (around 10) plus 3 tablespoons infused oil from the jar
3 teaspoons dried oregano
3 garlic cloves, peeled and crushed
4 spring onions (scallions)
250 g (9 oz) jarred artichokes in olive oil
large bunch (30 g/1 oz) basil
½–1 teaspoon sea salt flakes
½–1 teaspoon chilli flakes
200 g (7 oz) feta

SUBSTITUTES

—

Quick-cook farro
regular farro, pearl barley, brown rice, red rice, freekeh

Sundried tomatoes
jarred peppers, roasted cherry tomatoes, sunblush tomatoes

Basil
fresh oregano

Feta
mozzarella, goat's cheese

Peppers
leeks, spring onions (scallions)

TIP

—

This keeps really well if you make it ahead of time or for lunchboxes; just make sure you let it come back to room temperature before eating so that the flavours come back to life.

+   First, place the lemons in a medium pan along with the farro and bay leaves, if using. Top up the pan with water and boil on medium–high for 14–16 minutes, or until the farro is cooked but still tender. Drain in a colander and refresh under cold water for at least 30 seconds. Discard the bay, if using, spoon out the pips from the lemons and set aside to drain completely.

+   Meanwhile, slice the peppers as finely as you can (the finer they are, the sweeter they will become). Heat the oil from the jar of sundried tomatoes and the oregano in a large frying pan (skillet), add the peppers and garlic then gently fry in a single layer over a low medium heat for 10–12 minutes until really soft and sweet. Wash the spring onions, remove any tired-looking outer layers and trim away 2 cm (¾ in) from the green tops. Slice into thin rounds and add to the pan for the final minute of cooking. Remove the pan from the heat and allow to cool slightly.

+   Next, using kitchen paper, drain the excess oil from the sundried tomatoes and artichokes then slice lengthwise. Finely slice most of the basil (leaves and stalks), and then add to the peppers along with the tomatoes, artichokes and farro.

———— To assemble

Scoop the boiled lemon juice and flesh into the grains, sprinkle in ½ teaspoon of salt, ½ teaspoon of chilli flakes and most of the feta. Gently toss then taste; you may want to add more salt or chilli. Transfer to a large platter then crumble over the remaining feta. Pick over the reserved basil leaves to finish.

GRIDDLED SWEETCORN + AVOCADO SLAW

with

farro and harissa yoghurt

Charring a regular can of sweetcorn in a hot pan is a brilliant trick for adding a summery barbecue flavour to the kernels. Here, their natural sweetness pops through deep, rich, harissa-dressed grains, crunchy cabbage, smooth avocado and fragrant dukkah – a notch up on the classic coleslaw.

I use a quick-cook variety of farro from my local supermarket to add a chewy bite to this dish, but if you can't find any, regular farro or any substantial grain works just as well. Bear in mind, though, that it may need a few more minutes to prepare.

20 MINUTES

SERVES 4

140 g (5 oz) quick-cook farro
¼ teaspoon sea salt flakes
2 x 325 g (11½ oz) tins sweetcorn, rinsed and drained
1 tablespoon olive oil
1 teaspoon ground cumin
½ red cabbage (300 g/10½ oz)
2 carrots, peeled
large bunch (30 g/1 oz) coriander (cilantro), leaves only
large bunch (30 g/1 oz) flat-leaf parsley, leaves only
2 preserved lemons (optional)
2 ripe avocados, halved and stones removed
3 tablespoons dukkah (page 20; optional)

For the dressing:
1 garlic clove
25 g (1 oz) harissa paste (Belazu rose harissa is great)
200 g (7 oz) natural yoghurt
2 limes

SUBSTITUTES

—

Farro
pearl barley, brown rice, spelt

Avocado
griddled chicken or lamb kebabs

Red cabbage
sweetheart cabbage, white cabbage, spring greens

TIP

—

You can also char the avocados if you like. Simply place them flesh side down on the hot griddle pan for 3–4 minutes.

+ Bring a medium pan of water to the boil and carefully add the farro. Cook on a medium heat for the time stated on the packet (around 14–16 minutes) until tender but still chewy. Refresh under cold water in a colander, drain then set aside in a large mixing bowl along with the salt.

+ Heat a griddle pan or frying pan (skillet) until smoking. Add the sweet corn to the pan (you don't need any oil here) and cook for 3–5 minutes or until nicely charred with little black marks. Stir in the oil and cumin, cook for a further 30 seconds then transfer to a plate to cool.

+ Using the large side of a box grater, grate the cabbage and carrots. Roughly chop the coriander and parsley, and, if using, slice off the skin from the preserved lemons and finely slice (discard the flesh as it's salty and bitter).

+ Peel and crush the garlic then add to a small jug or bowl. Stir in the harissa, yoghurt and juice of 1 lime. Cut the remaining lime into 4 wedges.

——— To assemble

Toss the cabbage, carrots, herbs, preserved lemon peel (if using), harissa dressing and cooled sweetcorn through the farro then divide between four plates. Using a spoon, scoop half an avocado onto each plate. Scatter over the dukkah, if using, and serve with the lime wedges.

CHERRY, ALMOND + BAKED PITTA

with

pomegranate, chickpeas and mint

20 MINUTES

SERVES 4

SUBSTITUTES

—

Pomegranate molasses
honey mixed with a splash
of any kind of vinegar

Chickpeas (garbanzo beans)
cannellini, kidney,
butter (lima) beans

Sumac
lemon zest

Cherry and almond are flavours meant for each other, and here
I toss them through crunchy baked pitta for a new take on fattoush,
the popular Lebanese dish. Use fresh cherries if they are in season;
otherwise simply defrost some frozen ones.

I've used pomegranate molasses as I like the tart sweetness it adds
to the dressing, but if that's not in your cupboard, a splash of vinegar and
some honey will work just as well. If I'm making this as part of a larger
feast, I'll often serve it with some fried halloumi or hummus alongside.
The courgette fritters on page 140 make a great pairing as do the charred
prawns on page 46.

2 pitta or flatbreads (white or wholemeal)
1 tablespoon olive oil
1 teaspoon ground sumac
½ teaspoon ground cumin
¼ teaspoon sea salt flakes
50 g (2 oz) almonds
400 g (14 oz) tin chickpeas (garbanzo beans) in water, rinsed and drained
200 g (7 oz) cherries, stones removed and roughly chopped
large bunch (30 g/1 oz) flat-leaf parsley, roughly chopped
small bunch (20 g/¾ oz) mint, roughly chopped
130 g (4½ oz) radishes, sliced
2 large ripe tomatoes, deseeded and roughly chopped
1 small cucumber, deseeded and roughly chopped

For the dressing:
1 small garlic clove
2 teaspoons pomegranate molasses
juice of ½–1 lemon
1 tablespoon extra-virgin olive oil
1 teaspoon ground sumac

+ First, preheat the oven to 200°C (400°F/Gas 6). Open out the pitta, then
tear bite-size pieces into a baking tray and rub with the oil, sumac, cumin and
salt. Bake for 7 minutes then remove, give the tray a shake, add the almonds
and bake for another 3 minutes until the bread and almonds are golden.
(Keep an eye on them in the oven as I find oven temperatures and cooking
times really vary.) Transfer to a plate to cool.

———— To assemble

Peel and crush the garlic into a large mixing bowl then stir in the molasses,
juice of half the lemon, the oil and sumac. Slice the cooled almonds into
slivers then tip into the bowl along with the chickpeas, baked pitta and
remaining chopped ingredients. Toss gently to evenly coat in the dressing then
check the seasoning; you may want to squeeze in the remaining lemon half.
Serve immediately while the pitta is still nice and crunchy.

CHARRED COURGETTES + SWEETCORN

with

borlotti beans and lemon and basil pesto

20 MINUTES

SERVES 4

These days, courgette ribbons are often used as a replacement for pasta or noodles, but here I celebrate them as a fantastic vegetable in their own right. It may take you a few minutes to griddle the courgette ribbons in a single layer, but it's worth it for the intense, caramelised flavour.

The courgettes, sweetcorn and beans are dressed in my pesto from the go-to ingredients chapter; it's fresh and light and super-simple to make, but if you're pushed for time, just lighten some good-quality shop-bought stuff with a zest and squeeze of lemon juice.

2 large courgettes (zucchini)
1 tablespoon olive oil
325 g (11½ oz) tin sweetcorn in water, rinsed and drained
400 g (14 oz) tin borlotti (cranberry) beans in water, rinsed and drained
¼ teaspoon sea salt flakes
1 serving lemon and basil pesto (page 23)
small bunch (10 g/½ oz) basil (optional)

+ First, heat a large frying pan (skillet) or griddle pan until smoking. Next, using a speed peeler, create courgette ribbon lengths; stop once you reach the really seedy core and discard. Gently rub half of the oil into the ribbons then place in a single layer in the pan and cook for 2 minutes without interfering. (If the pan is too crowded to fit a single layer, cook the courgettes in two or three batches.) After 2 minutes, the courgettes should be starting to catch and nicely char; gently turn then cook for a further 2 minutes. Transfer to a plate to cool. Keep the pan on the heat.

+ Add the sweetcorn to the pan along with the remaining oil and fry for 3–5 minutes over a high heat until charred and blistered. (Some of the kernels may pop and dance in the pan, so take care.) Add the borlotti beans to the charred sweetcorn to warm through slightly. Stir in the salt then remove the pan from the heat and fold in the pesto.

———— To assemble

Transfer the beans and sweetcorn to a large platter. Lay the griddled courgettes on top then, if using, pick over the basil leaves to finish.

SUBSTITUTES

—

Borlotti (cranberry) beans
kidney, cannellini, butter (lima) beans

Lemon and basil pesto
basil oil (page 27), shop-bought pesto

TIP

—

When they're available, fresh borlotti (cranberry) beans, simmered until soft but still tender, make this dish extra special.

SAVOY CABBAGE, HERBY SAUSAGE + GARLIC CROUTONS

with

tomatoes, fennel and cannellini beans

Frying up rosemary-flecked sausage meat until it's golden and caramelised then tossing in sweet, ripe tomatoes and garlicky croutons has surely got to be one of the best ways to enjoy winter cabbage. This is a hearty supper inspired by the homely bean and vegetable soups you find in rural Italy, where a small amount of quality meat is made to go a very long way.

Italian-style sausages deliver quick flavour here as they're already mixed with the likes of rosemary, oregano, garlic, fennel seeds and black pepper. You could just use plain butcher's-quality sausages or chunky minced (ground) pork and fry in those classic Italian flavours yourself.

20 MINUTES

SERVES 4

1 small (400 g/14 oz) savoy cabbage
1 medium fennel bulb
3 tablespoons red wine vinegar
1 tablespoon extra-virgin olive oil
¼ teaspoon sea salt flakes
6 Italian-style pork sausages (see tip)
400 g (14 oz) tin cannellini beans in water, rinsed and drained
300 g (10½ oz) ripe tomatoes, at room temperature
small bunch (15 g/½ oz) flat-leaf parsley, leaves only
1 serving garlic sourdough croutons (page 19)
¼ teaspoon cracked black peppercorns or chilli flakes (optional)

+ First, wash the cabbage under cold water, pat dry, then finely shred (discard the tough inner core) and place in a large bowl. Slice the fennel lengthwise, as finely as you can (a mandolin is handy for this), then add to the bowl along with the vinegar, oil and salt. Using your hands, scrunch the vinegar and oil into the cabbage mix – this will help it soften and marinate.

+ Next, squeeze the sausage meat from its skins (discard the skins) and fry in a large non-stick pan over a high heat, using a wooden spoon to break the meat into chunks until golden brown, around 5–6 minutes. Stir the beans through the meat for the last 30 seconds of cooking – ensuring they pick up all the nice pork juices and caramelised flavours from the bottom of the pan.

———— To assemble

Roughly chop the tomatoes (aim for big, random shapes, not uniform dice) and parsley leaves, then add to the cabbage along with the sausage mix and croutons. Using a spoon, gently stir the salad until evenly combined and dressed. If using, crack over some black pepper or chilli flakes to finish. Serve immediately while the sausage meat is still warm.

SUBSTITUTES

—

Savoy cabbage
cavolo nero, kale, Chinese cabbage

Fennel
celery

TIP

—

If you can't get hold of Italian-style sausages, just buy high-quality plain pork sausages and add 1 crushed garlic clove plus a pinch of dried oregano, dried rosemary, chilli flakes, fennel seeds and ground black pepper when cooking.

WARM SPRING ONION + RED PEPPER FARRO

with

Manchego and almonds

20 MINUTES

SERVES 4

SUBSTITUTES

—

Spring onions
baby leeks or halved regular leeks, asparagus

Quick-cook farro
regular farro, spelt, pearl barley, freekeh, brown rice

Manchego
pecorino, Parmesan

Often I'll finely shred a few spring onions to add a subtle fresh note to a salad without overpowering it. But here, spring onions take centre stage, as once charred whole they go sweet and juicy.

The red pepper dressing is rich, smoky and velvety with just the right amount of punch coming in from the splash of vinegar. I'll quite happily eat it with some crusty bread while dreaming of holidays in Spain.

Here, the dressing goes beautifully with chewy farro grains and buttery Manchego. (See photo overleaf.)

200 g (7 oz) quick-cook farro
2 bay leaves (optional)
85 g (3 oz) flaked almonds
2 bunches (300 g/10½ oz) spring onions (scallions)
1 tablespoon olive oil, plus a drizzle
1 x 480 g (17 oz) jar roasted red (bell) peppers, drained
1 teaspoon tomato purée
½ garlic clove
75 g (2½ oz) Manchego
2 teaspoons smoked paprika
½ teaspoon red wine vinegar
pinch of sea salt flakes
small bunch (20 g/¾ oz) flat-leaf parsley, leaves only
100 g (3½ oz) wild rocket (arugula)

+ First, bring a medium pan of water to the boil then cook the farro and bay leaves, if using, for the time stated on the packet (around 10–12 minutes). Drain thoroughly, but don't rinse under cold water, then put in a large mixing bowl (discard the bay).

+ Meanwhile, toast the almonds in a large frying pan (skillet) over a high heat for 1–2 minutes, stirring regularly until golden, then transfer to a plate to cool. Keep the heat on high.

+ Next, wash the spring onions, remove any tired-looking outer layers and trim away 2 cm (¾ in) from the green tops. Rub the oil into the onions then cook in the hot pan with the lid on for 3 minutes until charred and blackened on one side. Remove the lid then, using tongs, turn the onions over and cook for a further 2–3 minutes with the lid back on. (Covering the pan means the onions will steam, making them go sweet and soft.) Transfer the onions to a plate and cover with the lid to continue steaming and keep them warm.

+ Add 250 g (9 oz) of the peppers to a food processor along with the tomato purée, garlic, 15 g (½ oz) of Manchego, paprika, vinegar, salt and 20 g (¾ oz) of the toasted almonds. Blend with a few splashes of water or a drizzle of oil until you get a pourable dressing consistency.

+ Finely slice the remaining peppers, roughly chop the parsley and slice half the cooked onions into 2 cm (¾ in) lengths. Wash the rocket in a basin of cold water (this will freshen and crispen the leaves) and pat dry.

Stir most of the dressing through the warm farro then carefully stir in the sliced peppers, parsley, sliced onions and rocket. Spoon onto a platter and top with the remaining almonds, onions and dressing. Finely grate or, using a speed peeler, shave over the remaining Manchego to finish.

Warm Spring Onion + Red Pepper Farro (page 62)

PICKLED WATERMELON + HALLOUMI SPELT

with

sundried tomatoes, sugar snap peas and mint

20 MINUTES

SERVES 4

SUBSTITUTES

—

Spelt
barley, farro, freekeh, couscous

Sugar snap peas
green beans, frozen peas

Halloumi
feta, Danish combi, salted ricotta
(don't fry these, though)

TIP

—

If your watermelon is on the large side,
why not scoop out and deseed the
leftover flesh then freeze and blend
into a slushie-style drink?

Watermelon is good mood food; brilliant eaten outside, somewhere warm and sunny. You'll see I quickly pickle the watermelon along with the red onion; not only to balance the salty halloumi and intense sundried tomatoes but because drawing out its naturally sweet juices helps to form a great dressing for the chewy spelt grains.

As is often the case, I go heavy on the herbs here, chopping a mix of parsley, dill and mint. By all means just use one or two kinds of soft herb if that's all you have to hand. Hopefully you'll agree this is a great dish to have in your collection for brighter days.

350 g (12 oz) spelt
3 tablespoons vinegar
1½ tablespoons sugar
½ teaspoon sea salt flakes
1 small red onion, peeled and halved
150 g (5 oz) sugar snap peas
6 jarred sundried tomatoes plus 2½ tablespoons infused oil from the jar
250 g (9 oz) halloumi
1 small watermelon (450 g/1 lb flesh)
200 g (7 oz) radishes, thinly sliced
small bunch (20 g/¾ oz) flatleaf parsley, leaves only
small bunch (20 g/¾ oz) dill, leaves only
small bunch (20 g/¾ oz) mint, leaves only
juice of 1 lime
3 tablespoons dukkah (page 20; optional)

+ First, bring a large pan of water to the boil and cook the spelt for the time stated on the packet (around 16–18 minutes). Then refresh under cold water, drain and set aside. Meanwhile, stir the vinegar, sugar and half the salt in a large bowl. Slice the onion into half-moons, as finely as you can, and stir through the vinegar mixture to quickly pickle (this will make the onion turn bright pink).

+ Next, fill a frying pan (skillet) 2 cm (¾ in) deep with water. Bring to a rapid boil then blanch the sugar snap peas over a high heat for 1 minute. Refresh under cold water, drain thoroughly then set aside.

+ Wipe out the pan with a few sheets of kitchen paper then heat 1 tablespoon of the sundried tomato oil over a high heat. Crumble in bite-size chunks of the halloumi (discarding any liquid from the packet) and fry for 3–4 minutes until golden. Set aside.

+ Chop the watermelon into large chunks (discarding the seeds and skin) and add to the onion pickle mixture for 5 minutes. Roughly chop the sundried tomatoes and finely chop the herbs.

——————— To assemble

Place the spelt, onion and pickled watermelon (not the pickling juice), sugar snap peas, remaining tomato oil, radishes, tomatoes, herbs and remaining salt in a large mixing bowl. Squeeze in the lime juice, gently toss with your hands so that everything is evenly distributed then transfer to a platter. Top with the halloumi and dukkah, if using.

PICKLED CAVOLO NERO, SOBA NOODLES + GINGER

with

sesame soft-boiled eggs

20 MINUTES

SERVES 4

SUBSTITUTES

—

Soba noodles
egg noodles, vermicelli noodles

Cavolo nero
savoy cabbage, spring greens

Fish sauce
soy sauce

This one is a favourite midweek supper at our place. Quickly pickling the cabbage is a vibrant way to pack in some greens, while the soba noodles are nutty yet comforting. Here, I've topped them with a perfectly cooked soft-boiled egg and toasted sesame seeds, but if you like a bit of heat, the chilli fried eggs on page 144 are a nice match.

I enjoy the bobbled, almost waxy texture of cavolo nero leaves, but have a play with any variety of cabbage or dark leafy greens to suit whichever season you're cooking in.

80 ml (2¾ fl oz) rice or white wine vinegar
2 tablespoons sugar (ideally white)
2 teaspoons fish sauce
200 g (7 oz) cavolo nero
4 eggs
200 g (7 oz) soba noodles
45 g (1½ oz) sesame seeds
2 large carrots
4 spring onions (scallions), finely shredded
20 g (¾ oz) fresh ginger, peeled and finely grated
60 ml (2 fl oz) toasted sesame oil
½ teaspoon chilli flakes (optional)

+ First, fill a medium pan with water and bring to the boil. In a medium bowl, stir together the vinegar, sugar and fish sauce until the sugar is mostly dissolved. Slice the cavolo nero lengthwise into ribbons 1 cm (½ in) wide (discard the tough inner core) then, using your hands, scrunch into the vinegar mix. Set aside to lightly pickle.

+ Carefully add the eggs to the pan of boiling water. Simmer on medium for 6 minutes then remove with a slotted spoon and plunge into a bowl of cold water to stop them cooking any further. (If you gently crack the base of the eggs just before you add to the cold water, they will be easier to peel.)

+ Next, add the noodles to the pan of water and cook over a high heat for the time stated on the packet (around 5 minutes). Refresh under cold water, drain thoroughly and place in a large mixing bowl.

+ Toast the sesame seeds in a small frying pan (skillet) over a high heat for 1–2 minutes until golden and you can smell the natural oils being released. Transfer to a plate to cool.

+ Top, tail and peel the carrots then, using a speed peeler, shave ribbon lengths.

Add the carrots, spring onions and ginger to the noodles along with the sesame oil and pickled cabbage (including 1 tablespoon of the pickling juice). Tip in most of the sesame seeds and toss until evenly coated. Check the seasoning; you may want to add a splash or two more of the pickling juice. Divide between 4 bowls. Peel the eggs then halve lengthwise and place on top of the noodles. Splash each egg yolk with some of the pickling juice, and scatter over the remaining sesame seeds and chilli flakes, if using.

KALE, APPLE + TARRAGON SLAW

with

candied pecans and capers

20 MINUTES

SERVES 4

SUBSTITUTES

—

Maple syrup
honey

Kale
savoy cabbage, cavolo nero

Tarragon
chopped rosemary

The added crunch in this slaw comes from toasting then candying the pecans for a few seconds in maple syrup then leaving them to cool until they become brittle. It's a simple technique you can do with any type of nut, not just to use in salads, but also to sprinkle on desserts, such as strained yoghurt or ice cream.

Here the pecan brittle combines with tart, crisp apple, salty capers and a creamy, aromatic, fried-tarragon mayo. It's a very pleasurable kale-based jumble.

75 g (2½ oz) pecan nuts
1 tablespoon maple syrup
250 g (9 oz) kale
1 teaspoon vinegar
2 teaspoons mayonnaise
150 g (5 oz) natural yoghurt
1 tablespoon olive oil
2 tablespoons capers, drained and crushed
small bunch (20 g/¾ oz) tarragon, leaves only
1 small fennel bulb
1 apple (ideally a tart, crisp variety like Granny Smith)
¼ teaspoon sea salt flakes (optional)

+ First, lay a sheet of non-stick baking paper on a plate. Using your hands, roughly crush the pecans into a small frying pan (skillet) over a high heat. Shake the pan regularly for 1–2 minutes or until you can smell the natural oils being released. Pour in the maple syrup, swirl the pan for 20–30 seconds (but don't stir) then transfer to the baking paper to cool and become brittle. (Don't get distracted at this point as the nuts and syrup can catch and burn quite easily.)

+ Next, wash the kale under cold water, pat dry and shred into 1 cm (½ in) strips (avoid and discard the tough stems). Place in a large mixing bowl and add the vinegar, mayonnaise and yoghurt then, using your hands, massage into the kale. Set aside to marinate and soften.

+ Clean and dry the frying pan and return it to a high heat. Add the oil to the hot pan, followed by the capers and tarragon. Fry for 1–2 minutes until the capers begin to pop and bloom. Transfer to a plate to cool.

+ Wash the fennel under cold water, pat dry then finely slice. Discard the tough inner core and reserve any leafy fronds. A mandolin is handy for this. Roughly chop the apple (don't bother peeling it) and discard the core. Roughly chop the cooled pecan brittle.

——————— To assemble

Toss the fennel, apple and most of the brittle through the dressed kale along with the capers and tarragon. Using your hands, gently mix until everything is evenly distributed then check the seasoning and add salt if needed (the capers are naturally salty so you may find it doesn't need extra). Transfer to a platter then scatter over the reserved brittle and any fennel fronds and serve/eat immediately.

RICE PAPER ROLLS
+ CASHEW SATAY

with

mint and coriander

I love how sociable this meal is. You just blend up the cashew satay, slice some veggies, place them on the table with the rice paper wrappers, then let everyone make up their own rolls. You could even keep a batch of satay on standby in the freezer then defrost it for whenever mates come round.

This recipe is a pure, basic version of rice paper rolls, so if I'm having people over, I like to offer a few other fillings. A pan of sticky sausage from my vermicelli noodles recipe (page 86) always goes down well, as do a couple of whole, fresh mackerel (page 139), simply grilled (broiled) then flaked at the centre of the table.

20 MINUTES

SERVES 4

150 g (5 oz) vermicelli rice noodles
1 large cucumber, deseeded
3 carrots, peeled
100 g (3½ oz) radishes, finely sliced
large bunch (30 g/1 oz) mint
large bunch (30 g/1 oz) coriander (cilantro)
12 large rice paper wrappers
1 serving cashew satay (page 20)

+   First, place the noodles in a large bowl. Cover with boiling water then set aside to soften for 10–15 minutes. Slice the cucumber and carrots into matchsticks and arrange on a nice serving plate along with the radishes and herbs.

+   Place the rice paper wrappers on the table together with a tray or dish filled with water. Drain the noodles and transfer to a large serving bowl for the table.

——— To assemble

To make a spring roll, take a wrapper and place it in the tray of water for a few seconds until it's pliable. Lay on a plate then layer up with the vegetables, herbs and a small handful of noodles. Fold the edge nearest you over the filling then tuck in the right and left sides. Keeping hold of the filling, roll away from you to form a spring roll then dip in the satay.

SUBSTITUTES

—

Rice paper wrappers
gem lettuce, steamed Chinese cabbage

Radish/cucumber/carrot
spring onions (scallions), beansprouts, cooked beetroot (beet), kohlrabi

CRISPY LAMB +
POPPADOM
CARROTS

with

cumin, chickpeas and pickled red onion

20 MINUTES

SERVES 4

A few store cupboard spices and some caramelised lamb mince transform a regular bunch of carrots into something pretty spectacular here.
This dish is full of great texture contrasts: crunchy poppadoms, smooth, cooling yoghurt, creamy chickpeas and that aromatic, spiced lamb; all of which is brought to life with pink pickled onion and a generous dollop of mango chutney.

½ red onion
2 limes
300 g (10½ oz) minced (ground) lamb (around 15–20% fat)
1 teaspoon mustard seeds
1½ teaspoons ground cumin
1 teaspoon ground coriander
¼ teaspoon ground cinnamon
½–1 teaspoon chilli flakes (depending on how spicy you like it)
¼ teaspoon sea salt flakes
4 carrots (a variety of colours is nice if you can get them)
6 small poppadoms
100 g (3½ oz) radishes, finely sliced
400 g (14 oz) tin chickpeas (garbanzo beans) in water, rinsed and drained
small bunch (20 g/¾ oz) coriander (cilantro)
2½ teaspoons olive oil
1 teaspoon honey
20 g (¾ oz) fresh ginger, peeled
150 g (5 oz) natural yoghurt
70 g (2½ oz) mango chutney

SUBSTITUTES
—

Lamb
minced (ground) beef,
chicken or pork,
firm marinated tofu

Chickpeas (garbanzo beans)
Bombay mix, sprouting pulses

Carrots
ripe tomatoes, radishes

+ First, peel the onion, slice into half-moons as finely as you can then place in a small bowl. (A mandolin is handy for this.) Squeeze in the juice of 1 lime then set aside to lightly pickle.

+ Next, put a large frying pan (skillet) over a high heat. Add the lamb and mustard seeds and cook for 5–6 minutes until dark and caramelised. (Take care as the mustard seeds will pop and dance in the pan.) Reduce the heat to low, add the cumin, ground coriander, cinnamon, chilli and salt then cook for a further minute. Turn off the heat but leave the pan on the hob so the lamb remains warmish.

+ Top, tail and peel the carrots then, using a speed peeler, shave ribbon lengths (stop once it gets too hard to peel the inner core and discard) and transfer to a platter. Roughly crush 2 of the poppadoms and scatter them over the carrots along with the radishes and chickpeas. Pick over the coriander leaves (discard the stalks).

+ By this stage, the onion should be bright pink and nicely pickled. Add the oil and honey to the bowl. Finely grate the ginger then squeeze in the juice (discard the grated root). Stir to combine.

———— To assemble

Scatter the onion over the carrots and, using your hands, gently toss, ensuring all the vegetables are coated in dressing (squeeze in a bit more lime if it feels too dry). Spoon over the warm crispy lamb to finish then serve at the table with the rest of the poppadoms, the yoghurt, mango chutney and wedges of the remaining lime.

A Quick Assembly (10–20 Minutes)

PEA + PARMA HAM FARFALLE

with

crispy rosemary, shallot dressing and cos lettuce

Frying cured meat in a hot pan so the fat renders out and becomes the base of a sharp vinaigrette was one of the first things my parents taught me in our kitchen as a child. Warm bacon salad was a weeknight staple in our house!

Here, instead of bacon lardons, I fry Parma ham until golden, throwing in a few sprigs of rosemary and making it go super-fragrant and crispy. Tossed through some classic farfalle, a handful of peas from the freezer and a fresh lettuce, this is food straight from my childhood and a recipe I come back to time and time again.

20 MINUTES

SERVES 4

200 g (7 oz) farfalle
250 g (9 oz) frozen peas
1 banana shallot or 2 small shallots, peeled and finely diced
3½ tablespoons extra-virgin olive oil
3 tablespoons red wine vinegar
1 teaspoon sugar
¼ teaspoon sea salt flakes
1 red cos (romaine) lettuce
6 slices (80 g/3 oz) Parma ham
2–3 sprigs (10 g/½ oz) rosemary, leaves only

+   First, bring a large pan of water to the boil. Carefully add the farfalle then cook for the time stated on the packet (around 12–14 minutes) until al dente. Add the peas to the pan for the last 1 minute of cooking then rinse under plenty of cold water, drain completely, transfer the pasta and peas to a large mixing bowl.

+   Put the shallots in a small jug or bowl and stir in 2½ tablespoons of the oil, the vinegar, sugar and salt then set aside. Wash the lettuce in a basin of cold water (this will freshen and crispen the leaves), pat dry then finely shred and set aside.

+   Next, put a large frying pan (skillet) over a high heat and add the slices of ham in a single layer. Cook for around 2 minutes on each side until golden and crisp, and some of the fat has rendered out of the ham, then transfer to a plate. Reduce the pan heat to medium. Roughly chop the rosemary and add to the hot pan with the remaining oil then cook for 1–2 minutes until crisp and fragrant. Stir in any sticky ham bits from the bottom of the pan.

——— To assemble

Toss the dressing and lettuce through the farfalle and peas. Tear in the cooked ham then stir to ensure everything is evenly coated. Scatter over the crispy rosemary to finish.

SUBSTITUTES

—

Farfalle
penne, fusilli, orecchiette, conchiglie pasta

Cos (romaine) lettuce
spinach, rocket (arugula)

Red wine vinegar
any vinegar variety

OREGANO HALLOUMI, TOMATOES + MINT YOGHURT

with

olives and cucumber

20 MINUTES

SERVES 4

SUBSTITUTES

—

Halloumi
feta, salted ricotta
(don't fry them)

Olives
capers, chopped anchovies

There's just something about fried halloumi – whenever you make it, people go wild for it. The irresistible combination of salty, chewy, warm cheese perhaps? I find marinating the halloumi for a few minutes in oregano and olive oil before frying takes things up a notch flavour-wise. Teamed with those Greek classics, olives, ripe tomatoes and mint yoghurt, it's unsurprising this goes down so well.

✓

250 g (9 oz) halloumi
1½ tablespoons olive oil
1½ teaspoons dried oregano
1 large cucumber
350 g (12 oz) ripe tomatoes
90 g (3 oz) pitted black olives jarred in brine (drained weight)
small bunch (10 g/½ oz) mint, leaves only
small bunch (10 g/½ oz) dill, leaves only
2½ teaspoons red wine vinegar
4 pitta breads (optional)

For the mint yoghurt dressing:
250 g (9 oz) natural yoghurt
1–1½ teaspoons dried mint
¼ teaspoon sea salt flakes
½–1 teaspoon honey
½ garlic clove, peeled and crushed

+ First, slice the halloumi into roughly 8 slices (discard any liquid from the packet) then place in a shallow bowl with the oil and oregano. Toss to coat then set aside to lightly marinate.

+ Next, to make the dressing, chop away a third of the cucumber then deseed and finely dice (reserve two-thirds of the cucumber for the next stage). Place in a medium bowl then stir in the yoghurt, 1 teaspoon dried mint, the salt and honey. Stir in the garlic then taste; you may want to add more dried mint. Set aside.

+ Roughly chop the tomatoes and the rest of the cucumber (aim for big, random shapes here, not uniform dice) then add to a large mixing bowl. Drain the olives then roughly tear in. Finely chop the mint and dill and add to the tomato mixture. Splash in the vinegar.

+ Fry the halloumi slices in a large frying pan (skillet) over a medium heat for 2 minutes on each side until golden and crisp at the edges then transfer to a plate. Pour any remaining oregano oil into the tomato mixture. If serving with pitta breads, warm them now.

———— To assemble

Toss the tomato mixture, ensuring it's evenly coated in oregano oil, vinegar and herbs. Take it to the table along with the mint yoghurt, halloumi and pitta breads, if using. Allow everyone to build their own salads.

WARM LEMON + FETA BEANS

with

chilli and toasted almonds

20 MINUTES

SERVES 4

I have my mum, Claire, to thank for most of my cooking ability; she's a wonder who can take a few sad-looking ingredients from a bare fridge and create something hearty and delightful within minutes. This was one of her unplanned dinners; a tin from the cupboard and a forgotten bunch of green beans brought to life with rosemary, garlic, lemon and feta.

Serve this with a chewy loaf of sourdough bread if you can as it's great for mopping up the citrussy juices. A few of my sweet potato and coriander fritters (page 141) are also lovely with this.

75 g (2½ oz) flaked almonds
4–5 large sprigs (20 g/¾ oz) rosemary, leaves only
3 garlic cloves
2 tablespoons extra-virgin olive oil
¼–½ teaspoon dried chilli flakes
450 g (1 lb) green beans, trimmed
juice of 1½ lemons
6 spring onions (scallions)
400 g (14 oz) tin butter (lima) beans in water, rinsed and drained
125 g (4 oz) feta, crumbled
4 slices (300 g/10½ oz) sourdough bread

+ First, toast the almonds for 2 minutes in a large frying pan (skillet) over a high heat until golden (stir frequently, taking care not to let them burn). Transfer to a plate to cool.

+ Next, finely chop the rosemary and garlic. Add to the pan along with the oil and chilli then cook over a medium heat for 2 minutes until fragrant (take care not to burn the garlic). Add the green beans plus enough water to cover them. Squeeze in the juice of the lemons (discard any pips) then boil over a high heat for 5–6 minutes, or until the beans are tender but retaining some bite.

+ While the beans are cooking, shred the spring onions by cutting them finely on an angle (discard any tough green upper layers). Using a slotted spoon, remove the cooked green beans from the pan and transfer to a large platter. Boil the pan water for another 2–3 minutes until reduced to a thick juice, and then stir in the spring onions and butter beans to warm for 30 seconds.

——— To assemble

Pour the spring onions, butter beans and pan juices over the platter of green beans. Scatter with the feta and toasted almonds to finish. Serve with the bread for mopping up the fragrant, lemony juices.

SUBSTITUTES

—

Green beans
runner beans

Butter (lima) beans
chickpeas (garbanzo beans), cannellini beans

Almonds
hazelnuts, pistachios, walnuts

BRAISED OLIVE + PUY LENTIL CASARECCE

with

garlic, lemon and radicchio

20 MINUTES

SERVES 4

I have my friend Hamish in Sydney to thank for the inspiration behind this seriously bold yet quick pasta salad. Dinner at Hamish's is never without his warm garlic and rosemary braised olives. This is a take on those but with radicchio and puy lentils thrown in for extra substance.

As the pasta and olives will positively mingle with the lemon, chilli and rosemary in the fridge, this one is great for making extras of, knowing that you've got some to enjoy in a lunchbox the next day. Just give it a chance to return to room temperature before tucking in.

200 g (7 oz) casarecce pasta
180 g (6 oz) jarred pitted kalamata olives in brine (drained weight)
3 tablespoons olive oil
½–1 teaspoon chilli flakes
¼–½ teaspoon sea salt flakes
2½ teaspoons sugar (ideally brown)
3 tablespoons red wine vinegar
3 sprigs rosemary, washed
3 garlic cloves
1 lemon
250 g (9 oz) sachet precooked puy lentils
1 small radicchio (200 g/7 oz)

+ First, bring a large pan of water to the boil. Carefully add the pasta then boil over a high heat for the time stated on the packet (around 10–12 minutes) until al dente then drain. Reserve a mugful of the cooking water.

+ Meanwhile, drain and rinse the olives then add to a large frying pan (skillet) along with the oil. Place over a medium heat then add ½ teaspoon of chilli, ¼ teaspoon of salt, the sugar, vinegar and rosemary (whole sprigs). Peel and bash the garlic then add to the pan. Using a speed peeler, create thin strips of lemon zest (avoid the bitter white pith) and add to the pan along with the juice of half the lemon. If the olives look to be drying out at any point, splash in some of the pasta cooking water to help them braise.

——— To assemble

Stir the cooked pasta into the olives along with the lentils. Remove any tired-looking outer leaves from the radicchio then finely shred and stir through the pasta. Increase the heat to high for 1 minute then remove. Have a little taste to check the seasoning. Depending on how naturally salty your olives are, you may want to add more salt, lemon juice or chilli flakes. Remove the woody rosemary talks then serve warm or at room temperature.

SUBSTITUTES

—

Casarecce
penne, trofie, farfalle, fusilli, orecchiette, conchiglie pasta

Kalamata olives
green or black olives

Rosemary
thyme, oregano

Radicchio
chicory (endive), wild rocket (arugula)

Red wine vinegar
white wine or cider vinegar, white or red wine, sherry

Puy lentils
tinned green lentils

Braised Olive + Puy Lentil Casarecce (page 78)

03

A
-
BIT MORE
TIME

25–45 MINUTES

The recipes in this chapter are all
really straightforward, but they need
just a few more minutes to develop big
flavour and interesting texture in the
oven or on the hob.

With most of them, you'll have
something special to serve up within
25–30 minutes. A few of the recipes
require slightly more patience but
don't take any longer than 45 minutes.

As with the salads in the previous
chapter, each feeds 4 comfortably as
a main meal. But they too have been
designed with the idea in mind that
you can serve them with some of the
other dishes from the book, forming
an even larger sharing feast.

MUSHROOM + ROSEMARY WILD RICE

with

crispy kale and garlic

25 MINUTES

SERVES 4

This is comforting autumnal food, without having to stand by the cooker for hours, waiting for something to reduce. (Although sometimes that act in itself can be a wonderful thing.) When it comes to cooking the mushrooms, be brave. Frying them in a really hot pan in a single layer will give them an intense, charred, almost meaty flavour. So if your pan is on the small side, it may be worth cooking the mushrooms in a few batches.

With cranberries bringing pops of sweetness and the wild rice a satisfying nuttiness, I'll happily serve bowls of this as it is, but an oozy poached egg on top would deliver an extra layer of comfort.

300 g (10½ oz/generous 1½ cups) wild rice
½ vegetable, chicken or beef stock cube (optional)
200 g (7 oz) kale
2 tablespoons olive oil
½ teaspoon sea salt flakes
40 g (1½ oz) blanched hazelnuts (see tip)
400 g (14 oz) mushrooms (ideally chestnut or wild mushrooms)
3–4 large sprigs (15 g/½ oz) rosemary, leaves only
3 garlic cloves, peeled and crushed
30 g (1 oz) dried cranberries or sour cherries
zest and juice of 1 lemon

+ First, preheat the oven to 180°C (350°F/Gas 4). Next, add the rice to a medium pan and top up with three times the volume of water. Crumble in the stock cube, if using, then bring to the boil and simmer over a medium–high heat for the time stated on the packet (around 18–20 minutes). Once cooked, refresh under cold water and drain.

+ Meanwhile, wash the kale under cold water and pat dry. Tear the leaves away from the tough stems and discard. Shred the kale into 1 cm (½ in) strips then add to a large roasting tray. Rub in 1 tablespoon of the oil and the salt then roast in a single layer for 7 minutes. (If the kale is overcrowded in the tray, it will steam rather than roast, so split across two if your trays are small.) Roughly crush the hazelnuts then add to one corner of the tray. Gently toss the kale then roast for a further 3–4 minutes until crisp and the hazelnuts are beginning to turn golden and release their natural oils. Set aside.

+ Put a large frying pan (skillet) over a high heat while you chop the mushrooms – thickly slice some, quarter others and leave any small mushrooms whole. Add to the hot pan along with ½ tablespoon of the oil and cook for 6 minutes, stirring now and again. (You want to let the mushrooms colour and catch to build up flavour rather than sweating and steaming them.) Finely chop the rosemary, reduce the pan heat to low and add the remaining ½ tablespoon of oil. Fry for 30 seconds. Remove from the heat and add the garlic to cook in the residual heat, stirring frequently so that it doesn't burn.

——— To assemble

Stir the cranberries, lemon zest and juice and rice into the mushrooms then gently toss. Scatter with the kale and hazelnuts to finish.

SUBSTITUTES

—

Wild rice
brown, red or white rice, buckwheat, quinoa

Kale
Kalettes, shredded Brussels sprouts, chard

Lemon
orange

TIP

—

Don't worry if your hazelnuts aren't blanched. Just rub the nuts between some sheets of kitchen paper when they come out of the oven. This will wipe away most of the papery skins.

VERMICELLI NOODLES, STICKY SAUSAGE + PICKLED RADISH

with

lemongrass, peanuts, mint and coriander

Please don't be put off by the number of ingredients in this recipe. You probably have quite a few of the items in your fridge or cupboard already and as this is such a crowd pleaser, I imagine that any new bottles of sauce you do buy will come in handy in the future.

This salad contains everything I love about Vietnamese food – silky-soft noodles, fresh herbs, vibrant pink pickles, a highly addictive lemongrass dressing, crunchy peanuts and sweet, sticky sausage that will transport you to the streets of Hanoi, where little plastic stools crowd the pavements outside *bún chả* eateries.

The sticky sausage is pretty memorable and quite a game-changer, but if sausage isn't for you, just use some firm tofu or smoked mackerel instead. This goes perfectly with a cold beer or iced lemon tea. (See photo overleaf.)

30 MINUTES

SERVES 4

200 g (7 oz) vermicelli rice noodles
6 pork sausages
2 tablespoons hoisin sauce
1 tablespoon Sriracha chilli sauce
5 spring onions (scallions), finely shredded
2 baby gem lettuces, finely shredded
100 g (3½ oz) unsalted roasted peanuts
small bunch (20 g/¾ oz) mint
small bunch (20 g/¾ oz) coriander (cilantro)

For the pickled radish:
80 ml (2¾ fl oz) vinegar
2 tablespoons sugar (ideally white)
½ tablespoon fish sauce
200 g (7 oz) radishes, finely sliced

For the dressing:
2 lemongrass stalks
3 garlic cloves, peeled and crushed
½–1 small red chilli (depending on how spicy you like it), finely sliced
1½ tablespoons sugar (ideally white)
zest and juice of 3 limes
1½ tablespoons fish sauce
1 tablespoon toasted sesame oil

SUBSTITUTES

—

Sausages
smoked mackerel, firm tofu, tempeh

Fish sauce
sea salt flakes

Lemongrass
ginger, galangal

Peanuts
cashews, almonds

Radish
carrot, mooli (daikon), kohlrabi

+   First, put a full kettle on to boil.

+   To make the pickle, stir together the vinegar, sugar and fish sauce in a medium bowl. Add the radishes and leave aside to lightly pickle.

+   Place the noodles in a large bowl and cover with the boiling water from the kettle, reserving a few tablespoons in the kettle for the dressing. Leave for 5–10 minutes until soft then refresh under plenty of cold water, drain and set aside.

+   Next, prepare the dressing. Remove the tough outer layers of the lemongrass, finely slice then place in a small jug. Add a tablespoon of boiling water, along with the garlic, chilli, sugar, most of the lime zest and juice, fish sauce and sesame oil. Stir well and taste for a happy balance of hot, sour, salty and sweet; you may want to add more lime.

+   Next, place a non-stick frying pan (skillet) over a high heat. Remove the sausages from their skins (discard the skins) and add to the pan. Roughly break up the meat with a wooden spoon and cook for 5 minutes until really brown and caramelised. Stir in the hoisin and Sriracha sauce, then turn off the heat.

————— To assemble

Toss most of the dressing through the drained noodles and divide between four large bowls or arrange on a large platter. Top with the sausage meat, spring onions, lettuce, peanuts and pickles (including a splash of the pickling juice). Pick over half the mint and coriander leaves (discard the stalks). Take the remaining dressing and herbs to the table for people to add more if they fancy.

Vermicelli Noodles, Sticky Sausage + Pickled Radish (page 86)

ORANGE
CARROT
FREEKEH

with

cranberries and walnuts

25 MINUTES

SERVES 4

SUBSTITUTES

—

Freekeh
brown rice, quinoa, pearl barley

Carrots
radishes, precooked
beetroots (beets)

Cranberries
sultanas (golden raisins), sour cherries

I first had a salad like this at a sun-drenched cafe in Melbourne on a hot summer's day. Like most food (and drink) served in the city's cafes, it was fresh, bright and inspiring, although the mix of orange, cranberries and walnuts did remind me of dark Christmas nights in Scotland.

Still, it's a cracking and memorable flavour combination and one to keep in mind for whenever roast carrot kind of weather arrives wherever you are. Leftovers can easily be popped in a tub for lunch the next day.

200 g (7 oz) freekeh
zest and juice of 1 orange
½ teaspoon sea salt flakes
40 g (1½ oz) walnuts
5 carrots, peeled or 300 g (10½ oz) baby carrots
1 tablespoon olive oil
20 g (¾ oz) fresh ginger, peeled and finely grated
small bunch (20 g/¾ oz) dill, leaves only
1½ teaspoons red wine or cider vinegar
30 g (1 oz) dried cranberries

+ First, place the freekeh in a medium pan. Top up with three times the volume of water, bring to the boil then cook over a high heat until tender but still retaining some bite (check the packet instructions for exact cooking times, around 13–15 minutes). Refresh under plenty of cold water, drain then transfer to a large mixing bowl. Stir in the orange zest and salt.

+ Meanwhile, toast the walnuts in a large frying pan (skillet) over a high heat for 1–2 minutes until fragrant and releasing their natural oils. Transfer to a plate to cool. Next, slice the carrots into 2 cm (¾ in) thick coins on an angle. (If using baby carrots, as pictured, leave them whole.) Heat the oil in the frying pan then cook the carrots for 2 minutes until beginning to colour at the edges. Pour in 120 ml (4 fl oz) of water and the orange juice then add the ginger and boil for 4–5 minutes, or until the water has evaporated into a sticky glaze. Remove from the heat and set aside to cool slightly.

——— To assemble

Finely chop the dill and walnuts then toss through the freekeh along with the vinegar and cranberries. Transfer to a large platter then top with the sticky carrots and glaze to finish.

PICKLED FENNEL, WHIPPED MINT RICOTTA + BROAD BEANS

with

garlic croutons and sugar snap peas

25 MINUTES

SERVES 4

SUBSTITUTES

—

Broad beans
peas, edamame beans

Fennel
kohlrabi, celery

Ricotta
goat's curd, mascarpone,
cream cheese

Quickly pickling fennel shavings in freshly squeezed lemon and a few pinches of sugar tones down the bulb's aniseedy notes, making it a delight in this springtime tumble of broad beans and sugar snap peas.

Blending ricotta along with lemon zest and mint until it's really airy and spreadable makes it just the thing for topping with garlic croutons and the light greens.

I've recommend frozen broad beans for ease here, but if you can get them in season, podding fresh ones and popping them from their skins makes for therapeutic kitchen time.

2 lemons
2 teaspoons sugar (ideally white)
1 medium fennel bulb
150 g (5 oz) frozen broad (fava) beans
200 g (7 oz) sugar snap peas
small bunch (15 g/½ oz) mint, leaves only
250 g (9 oz) ricotta
¾ teaspoon sea salt flakes
120 g (4 oz) radishes, finely sliced
1 serving garlic sourdough croutons (page 19)
1½ tablespoon extra-virgin olive oil

+ First, zest the lemons and set aside (the zest will be used for flavouring the ricotta later). Squeeze the juice of 1½ lemons into a bowl then stir in the sugar until it mostly dissolves. Slice the fennel lengthwise, as finely as you can (discard the tough inner core) – a mandolin is handy for this – and set aside in the lemon mixture to quickly pickle.

+ Next, bring a medium pan of water to the boil then cook the broad beans over a high heat for 3 minutes. Add the sugar snap peas to the pan and cook for a further minute. Refresh the beans and sugar snap peas under lots of cold water until they're chilled then drain and pat dry with kitchen paper. Pop most of the broad beans from their thick skins, keeping some intact.

+ Add half the mint leaves to a food processor along with the ricotta, lemon zest and salt. Blitz until the ricotta is smooth and flecked with shredded mint.

——— To assemble

Smear the whipped ricotta onto a large platter or across four plates. Layer up with the pickled fennel (discard the pickle juice), beans, sugar snap peas, radishes and croutons. Drizzle over the oil and squeeze over the remaining lemon half. Scatter with the rest of the mint to finish.

ROAST
TOMATO ORZO

with

dukkah and thyme

25 MINUTES

SERVES 4

Your oven does all the hard work in this recipe, turning the tomatoes all burnished, sticky and intensely sweet. And like most roast tomato dishes, the flavours get even better with time, so this is a nice option if you need to make something hearty in advance.

A scattering of dukkah brings a smoky, spiced crunch to the silky orzo pasta. I like to make my own jar of dukkah (page 20) to have at hand for different salads and eggs in the morning, but if that sounds like too much forward planning, most supermarkets sell a version. Keep in mind there's salt in the dukkah that will season the orzo; you'll probably find it doesn't need much more.

600 g (1 lb 5 oz) ripe cherry tomatoes
small bunch (15 g/½ oz) thyme, leaves only
2 tablespoons olive oil
½ teaspoon sea salt flakes
¼ teaspoon cracked black pepper
½ teaspoon chilli flakes (optional)
1 teaspoon ground cumin
2 large garlic cloves
300 g (10½ oz) orzo
large bunch (30 g/1 oz) flat-leaf parsley, leaves only
1 lemon
3 tablespoons dukkah (page 20; optional)

+ First, preheat the oven to 220°C (425°F/Gas 7) and bring a medium pan of water to the boil. Slice the tomatoes, some in halves, some in quarters, then add to a large roasting tray in a single layer. Scatter over the thyme leaves and add the oil, salt, pepper, chilli flakes (if using), cumin and garlic (leave the skins on). Gently toss and roast for 15 minutes. Remove and reserve the garlic then roast the tomatoes for a further 5 minutes until starting to catch at the edges.

+ Meanwhile, boil the orzo in the pan of water over a medium heat for the time stated on the packet (around 8–10 minutes for al dente). Refresh under cold water to stop the pasta cooking then drain completely. Roughly chop the parsley leaves.

——— To assemble

Squeeze the roasted garlic flesh into the roasting tray. Using a fork, mash the garlic and half of the tomatoes into a chunky pulp. Add the cooked orzo into the tray then zest in the lemon. Squeeze in the juice of half the lemon then taste; you may want to add more lemon depending on the acidity/sweetness of your tomatoes. Add the parsley then stir everything together, ensuring you scrape all the nice sticky bits off the bottom of the tray. Transfer to a large platter then scatter with the dukkah, if using, to finish.

SUBSTITUTES

—

Thyme
rosemary, oregano

Orzo
mini pasta shells,
spelt, freekeh

HOT + SOUR CHICKEN IN GEM LETTUCE

with

roasted rice, mint and cucumber

25 MINUTES

SERVES 4

The year I spent at university in Bangkok was a special one. I was there to study business, but really, the best education I got was in the markets and streets from the hawkers selling the finest food in the country – everything from steaming bowls of noodles to whole lobsters charred over hot coals. This was one of my favourite dishes to order: a lively north-eastern Thai-Lao dish of hot and sour minced meat served in individual lettuce leaves.

It may seem a bit strange me asking you to toast and grind rice here, but please don't skip this step as it's the toasty, almost popcorn-like aromas that really make this dish so well-rounded.

50 g (2 oz/¼ cup) rice (white or brown)
500 g (1 lb 2 oz) skinless chicken breasts
2 tablespoons vegetable oil
½–1 teaspoon chilli flakes
2 tablespoons fish sauce
½ teaspoon sugar (ideally white)
3 limes
1 small red onion
small bunch (15 g/½ oz) mint, leaves only
6 spring onions (scallions)
½ cucumber or 2 baby cucumbers
2 baby gem lettuces

+ First, cook the rice in a large frying pan (skillet) over a high heat for 6–7 minutes, stirring occasionally until golden, toasted and smelling like popcorn. Add to a food processor then blitz until you get a rough power. Transfer to a small plate and set aside.

+ Next, blitz the chicken until minced (don't worry if there's some rice dust left in the processor). Add the oil to the pan and cook the chicken for 4–5 minutes over a high heat until it turns white and begins to golden. Remove from the heat then stir in most of the ground rice, ½ teaspoon of chilli flakes, the fish sauce and sugar. Zest in the limes then squeeze in the juice of 2½ limes. Allow to cool.

+ Peel the onion then slice into half-moons as finely as you can. Finely shred the mint leaves and spring onions (discard any tough outer leaves). Using a speed peeler, create cucumber lengths until you reach the seeds (discard the inner flesh and seeds). Add the sliced onion and most of the mint and spring onion to the cooled chicken (reserve some mint leaves and spring onion for garnish). Taste; you may want to add more chilli and lime juice.

———— To assemble

Wash the lettuce in a basin of cold water (this will freshen and crispen the leaves), pat dry then cut away the bases. Lay individual leaves on a large platter then top each leaf with a few cucumber ribbons and a large spoonful of chicken. Scatter over the reserved ground rice, mint and spring onions to finish.

SUBSTITUTES

—

Baby gem
chicory (endive)

Chicken
minced (ground) pork,
peeled raw prawns (shrimps)

Mint
coriander (cilantro), Thai basil

TIP

—

Freeze the inner discarded cucumber for popping into gin and tonics.

WARM DILL LENTILS

with

cumin spinach and yoghurt

This is one of those great, quick, one-pan dinners that delivers big on flavour but with minimal fuss. While I throw it together, I leave the others to set the table; then, when it's ready, I just place it down in the middle and let everyone dig in.

Tinned lentils are such a store cupboard hero for speeding up your cooking, and here they not only provide hearty substance but are a great carrier for cumin-spiced spinach and braised dill.

If you've got more time to spare, serving this with my harissa roast chicken (page 137), some warm flatbreads, hummus and a few pickled radishes makes a delicious feast.

25 MINUTES

SERVES 4

2 onions
3 tablespoons olive oil
¼–½ teaspoon sea salt flakes
2 garlic cloves, peeled and crushed
3 teaspoons ground cumin
200 g (7 oz) spinach
large bunch (30 g/1 oz) dill, roughly chopped
2 x 390 g (13¾ oz) tins green lentils in water, rinsed and drained
1 lemon
3 tablespoons natural yoghurt

+ First, peel and slice the onion into half-moons, as finely as you can. Put the oil in a large frying pan (skillet) then cook the onion with ¼ teaspoon of salt over a low heat for 8 minutes. Add the garlic and cumin and cook for a further 5–6 minutes until the onion is really soft and sweet.

+ Meanwhile, rinse the spinach under plenty of cold water and drain completely, squeezing out any excess moisture. Add the dill to the onion along with the drained lentils and spinach. Zest in the lemon and squeeze in the juice of half, then increase the heat to high. Cover with a lid and steam for 1 minute until the greens are wilted but still retain some shape. Check the seasoning; you may want to add more salt and lemon juice.

———— To assemble

Drizzle and swirl the yoghurt over the lentils then serve warm at the table in the pan.

SUBSTITUTES

—

Green lentils
precooked puy lentils,
bulgur wheat, spelt, brown rice

Spinach
kale, chard, cavolo nero

Onions
leeks, spring onions (scallions)

Dill
parsley, tarragon

Yoghurt
feta, ricotta

WARM CHARD, MANGO + CRISPY PANEER

with

mustard seeds, potatoes, coriander chutney and cashews

25 MINUTES

SERVES 4

SUBSTITUTES

—

Rainbow chard
kale, cavolo nero,
large leaf spinach

Cashews
almonds, coconut flakes

Chard's dark green leaves make it ideal for carrying tempered spices like the mustard seeds here. Inspired by the fantastic Indian flavours we got to experience growing up in east London, this chard is tossed through fluffy new potatoes, a spicy coriander and toasted cashew dressing, lime-dressed mango and fried paneer. It makes for a very happy dinner.

If you can spot it in the markets, and increasingly the supermarkets, the neon, rainbow variety of chard makes cooking this dish that extra bit special.

400 g (14 oz) new potatoes
60 g (2 oz) cashews
small bunch (20 g/¾ oz) mint, leaves only
2 large bunches (60 g/2 oz) coriander (cilantro)
1 green chilli
2 limes
pinch of sea salt flakes
1 small ripe mango
300 g (10½ oz) rainbow chard or silver beet
2½ tablespoons vegetable oil
2 teaspoons mustard seeds
2 garlic cloves, peeled and crushed
220 g (7½ oz) paneer

+ First, bring a large pan of water to the boil. Carefully add the potatoes then simmer over a medium heat for around 15–18 minutes or until tender all the way through – you can check by inserting a sharp knife. Drain in a colander and allow to steam.

+ Meanwhile, toast the cashews in a large frying pan (skillet) for 1–2 minutes to release their natural oils. Set aside half (for garnish later) and place the other half in a food processor along with the mint, coriander, chilli, zest and juice of 1 lime and salt until smooth. Transfer to a large mixing bowl.

+ Next, peel the mango and roughly slice (discard the large stone). Transfer to a plate, squeeze over the juice of the remaining lime then set aside. Wash the chard under cold water, pat dry then roughly chop. Put 1 tablespoon of the oil in the frying pan over a medium heat then add the mustard seeds and fry for 1 minute until they begin to pop. Add the garlic, fry for 30 seconds then add the chard. Fry for 2 minutes then remove from the heat.

——— To assemble

Roughly chop the warm potatoes into large dice then toss through the bowl of coriander chutney along with the chard. Put the pan back over a high heat, add the remaining oil then crumble in the paneer. Fry for 2–3 minutes, or until crispy, then spoon onto the dressed chard mixture along with the limey mango and reserved cashews.

CHARRED BROCCOLI, FLATBREADS + HARISSA CHICKPEAS

with

charred lemon and yoghurt

25 MINUTES

SERVES 4

SUBSTITUTES

—

Purple sprouting broccoli
broccoli florets, broccolini, Brussels sprouts, sugar snap peas, asparagus

Chickpeas (garbanzo beans)
cannellini beans

Yoghurt
feta, goat's curd, hummus

Caramelising the lemons while you cook the broccoli will soften their tart juice, giving a bright lift to this effortless jumble of charred flatbread, chickpeas and parsley. With a spoonful of yoghurt to cool the harissa's rich, smoky heat, there's little wonder this dish has become a lunchtime favourite in our house.

250 g (9 oz) purple sprouting or tender-stem broccoli
2 pitta breads or medium khobez flatbreads
1½–2 tablespoons olive oil
2 lemons, halved
400 g (14 oz) tin chickpeas (garbanzo beans) in water, rinsed and drained
2–3 teaspoons harissa paste (Belazu rose harissa is great)
small bunch (15 g/½ oz) flat-leaf parsley, leaves only, roughly chopped
sea salt flakes (optional)
100 g (3½ oz) thick natural yoghurt

+ First, bring a medium pan of water to the boil. Halve any thicker broccoli stems lengthwise then boil over a high heat for 3 minutes. Refresh under cold water and drain.

+ Meanwhile, preheat a griddle pan or frying pan (skillet) until smoking. Toast the flatbreads over a high heat for 1–2 minutes each side or until beginning to char. (You can also cook it by carefully placing directly over an open flame using tongs.) Set aside to cool slightly then cut into 5 mm (¼ in) strips.

+ Rub 1½ tablespoons oil over the broccoli then char for 4 minutes in the same pan over a high heat, tossing now and again. Add the lemons to the pan, cut side down, alongside the broccoli until charred and caramelised.

——— To assemble

Place the chickpeas, flatbreads and 2 teaspoons of harissa in a large mixing bowl. Add the parsley leaves then the broccoli. Using tongs, squeeze in the juice from 3 lemon halves (discard any pips). Gently toss to combine then check the seasoning; you may want to add more harissa, lemon juice, oil or some salt. (I find different harissa brands vary in saltiness, so it's best to taste first). Once you're happy with the balance of flavours, divide between four plates then serve with a dollop of yoghurt to finish.

DILL PICKLE POTATOES

with

caper mayonnaise and pickled red onion

Creamy and rich as you'd expect a potato salad to be, but with the added vibrancy of pickled red onion, chopped gherkins and dill, this is my take on the classic. I adore spooning this onto a slice of rye or crispbread to eat with cured salmon, herring or crayfish and some grated beetroot.

The dressed potatoes lend themselves to being made ahead of time for barbecues and lunches – just make sure you give them an hour or so out of the fridge before eating so that the flavours have a chance to come back to life.

Have a taste before adding lots of seasoning; I find the capers and pickled red onion alone bring enough saltiness.

25 MINUTES

SERVES 4

600 g (1 lb 5 oz) new potatoes
1 small red onion
juice of 1 lemon
¼–½ teaspoon sea salt flakes
1 tablespoon capers, drained and finely chopped
75 g (2½ oz) gherkins (in dill vinegar if you can get them), drained and finely chopped
small bunch (25 g/1 oz) dill, leaves only
3 tablespoons mayonnaise

+ First, bring a large pan of water to the boil. Carefully add the potatoes and simmer over a medium heat for around 15–18 minutes or until tender all the way through – you can check by inserting a sharp knife. Drain in a colander and allow to steam.

+ Meanwhile, peel and slice the onion into half-moons as finely as you can, then transfer to a small bowl. Squeeze over the lemon (discard any pips), stir in ¼ teaspoon of salt then set aside to lightly pickle.

+ Next, put the capers and gherkins in a large mixing bowl. Finely chop most of the dill leaves (reserve a few leaves for garnish), add to the bowl then stir in the mayonnaise.

——— To assemble

Roughly chop the potatoes while still warm then toss in the mayonnaise dressing. Add the onion (discard the pickling juice) then check the seasoning (I find the capers deliver enough saltiness, but you may want to add more salt). Scatter over the reserved dill leaves to finish.

SUBSTITUTES

—

Red onion
white onion, shallots, spring onions (scallions)

Dill
flat-leaf parsley, chervil, tarragon

Mayonnaise
natural yoghurt

PICKLED RHUBARB + SESAME BEETROOT

with

watercress and ginger

25 MINUTES

SERVES 4

SUBSTITUTES

—

Rhubarb
cherries, plums

Watercress
rocket (arugula), Japanese greens,
red butterhead lettuce

Tossing a vegetable in some acid to quickly transform it into a quick pickle is one of my favourite ways to inject vibrancy into a meal. Here it's rhubarb I'm pickling, as the sweet and sour slices of pink stem cut so nicely through the earthy beetroot. With a full-on ginger and sesame dressing, this is a salad for those times when you need to be awakened and inspired by the meal you're eating.

If you're looking for a bigger accompaniment to try this with, the rhubarb cuts brilliantly through anything that's naturally oily or fatty. Think roasted pork belly, oily fish like grilled mackerel (page 139), as pictured, or a simple but delicious chilli fried egg (page 144).

80 ml (2¾ fl oz) vinegar
2 tablespoons sugar (ideally white caster)
½ teaspoon sea salt flakes
2–3 rhubarb stalks (150 g/5 oz)
4 spring onions (scallions)
40 g (1½ oz) sesame seeds
25 g (1 oz) fresh ginger, peeled and finely grated
2½ tablespoons toasted sesame oil
80 g (3 oz) watercress
250 g (9 oz) raw beetroots (beets) (around 2 medium beetroots;
    use different colours if you can)
300 g (10½ oz) precooked beetroots (beets), at room temperature

+ First, stir together the vinegar, sugar and salt in a medium bowl. Slice the rhubarb as finely as you can (a mandolin is handy for this if you have one), then toss in the vinegar mixture. Set aside for 10 minutes to lightly pickle.

+ Meanwhile, shred the spring onions by cutting them finely on an angle (discard any tough green upper layers). Place them in a small bowl of cold water (this softens their flavour when eating them raw) and set aside. Next, toast the sesame seeds in a small frying pan (skillet) over a high heat for 1–2 minutes, until fragrant and golden, then transfer to a plate to cool.

+ Put the ginger in a small jug or bowl, and stir in the sesame oil plus 3 tablespoons of the rhubarb pickling juice.

+ Wash the watercress in a basin of cold water (this will freshen and crispen the leaves), pat dry and scatter over a large platter. Using a speed peeler, peel the raw beetroots then slice into rounds as finely as you can. Repeat with the cooked beetroots (a mandolin is handy for getting really thin rounds) then scatter the beetroots over the watercress.

———— To assemble

Drain the spring onions, squeezing out any excess water with your hands, then scatter over the beetroots along with the pickled rhubarb (not the pickling juice) and toasted sesame seeds. Drizzle over the sesame oil mixture to finish. Gently toss then serve and eat immediately while the leaves are crisp.

SHREDDED MANGO, LIME + PEANUTS

with

tomatoes and chilli

This on its own, or with whole grilled fish and jasmine rice, was our go-to lunch at the university canteen in Bangkok. If you ever get the chance to visit, it's worth joining the crowds of students on the Chulalongkorn campus, just to experience their incredible standard of canteen cooking. It's open to the public and they'll happily feed you with some of the best food you've ever tasted for just a few Baht.

I've left the quantities for chilli and lime quite open here; as with Thai food generally, it's all about personal preference and regularly tasting then re-tasting until you get the balance of hot, sour, salty and sweet that's spot-on for you. If you fancied having it with fish, the grilled mackerel on page 139 is a great match.

25 MINUTES
(15 WITHOUT THE RICE)
SERVES 4

180 g (6 oz/1 cup) white or brown rice (optional)
85 g (3 oz) unsalted peanuts
1 garlic clove
1–2 chillies
juice of 2–3 limes
2 tablespoons brown sugar
2 tablespoons fish sauce
180 g (6 oz) ripe cherry tomatoes, at room temperature
2 large green, unripe mangoes (1.2kg/2 lb 10 oz), peeled
1 carrot, peeled
small bunch (10 g/½ oz) coriander (cilantro), leaves only

+ If serving with rice, cook this first in a large pan of boiling water. Check the packet instructions for exact timings, around 18–20 minutes, then drain and set aside.

+ Toast the peanuts in a small frying pan (skillet) over a high heat for 2–3 minutes until fragrant and releasing their natural oils. Set aside on a plate to cool.

+ Next, peel and bash the garlic and 1 chilli (seeds included) in a pestle and mortar until it forms a rough paste (see tips). Add the juice of 2 limes, the sugar and fish sauce, then stir and taste. You're aiming for a balance of hot, sour, salty and sweet. You may want to add more lime juice or chilli to taste.

+ Halve the tomatoes and place in a large bowl. Use a julienne peeler (see tips) to create thin strips of the mango (discard the stone) and carrot, and then add to the tomatoes.

——— To assemble

Toss the dressing through the tomatoes, mango and carrot. Transfer to a large platter then scatter over the cooled peanuts and coriander. Serve and eat immediately (with the rice, if using) while the vegetables are still crunchy.

SUBSTITUTES

—

Peanuts
unsalted cashews, almonds

Fish sauce
sea salt flakes

TIP

—

Don't worry if you haven't got a pestle and mortar; just finely chop and crush the chilli and garlic using the side of your knife then stir with the lime juice, sugar and fish sauce in a small bowl.

If you don't have a julienne peeler, use a speed peeler to create ribbons then finely slice lengthwise to create long, thin strips.

CASHEW SATAY, POTATOES + TOMATOES

with

beansprouts, radishes and coriander

25 MINUTES

SERVES 4

I return to my Cashew Satay from page 20 to make these versatile veggie-packed bowls. It was years ago in Indonesia where I first sampled a dish like this; a lady had set up on the beach with her heavy-granite pestle and mortar, grinding the nuts by hand before tossing in fresh vegetables that she'd cycled back from the market early that morning. It was pretty special.

Have a play with whichever veggies are available and in season when making this dish; as long as you've got some that are crunchy and a touch of citrus to balance the soft potato and boiled egg, you can't go wrong. I've kept the prawn crackers optional but seriously recommend dipping them into that cashew sauce.

300 g (10½ oz) new potatoes
1 teaspoon sea salt flakes
150 g (5 oz) ripe cherry tomatoes, at room temperature
100 g (3½ oz) radishes
1 grapefruit
1 serving cashew satay (page 20)
200 g (7 oz) beansprouts
150 g (5 oz) sugar snap peas
small bunch (15 g/½ oz) coriander (cilantro)
4 hard-boiled eggs, halved (page 144; optional)
1 lime, quartered
bag of prawn crackers (optional)

+ First, bring a large pan of water to the boil. Carefully add the potatoes and salt then simmer over a medium heat for around 15–18 minutes or until tender all the way through – you can check by inserting a sharp knife. Drain in a colander and allow to steam.

+ Next, roughly chop the tomatoes and radishes into different shapes (aim for big, random shapes, not uniform dice). Slice the top and bottom off the grapefruit, then carefully cut away the peel and white pith. Slice into segments or large chunks.

——— To assemble

Grab 4 bowls and spread a few spoonfuls of satay sauce across the bottom. Roughly chop the potatoes then divide them between the bowls. Layer up with the tomatoes, radishes, raw beansprouts, sugar snap peas and grapefruit. Pick over the coriander leaves (discard the stalks), top with egg halves, if using, and serve with the lime wedges and some prawn crackers, if you fancy.

SUBSTITUTES

—

New potatoes
brown rice, jasmine rice

Grapefruit
unripe mango

Sugar snap peas
green beans, asparagus

TIP

—

I've found when making the satay that carton sizes of coconut cream vary greatly. So if you've got some cream left over, squeeze in some honey then freeze it for dessert.

CRISPY CHICKPEAS + PARSLEY MAFTOUL COUSCOUS

with

hummus and pickles

30 MINUTES

SERVES 4

SUBSTITUTES

—

Maftoul
bulgur wheat, giant couscous, regular couscous, freekeh

Radishes
cucumber, carrots

TIP

—

If you want your radishes to turn bright pink like the pickled turnips you see in kebab shops, add in some chopped beetroot to help stain them.

At first glance, this may look like a long list of ingredients, but I promise the recipe is very straightforward and worth it. The star of the show is the couscous, stirred through masses of finely chopped parsley like you'd find in a tabbouleh. I've used Fairtrade maftoul, an increasingly popular Palestinian bulgur wheat that's slightly larger than couscous. Use the regular stuff if that's easier. Topped with crispy chickpeas, with a bowl of pickled radishes and silky-smooth hummus, this is perfect for sharing.

For the crispy chickpeas:
400 g (14 oz) tin chickpeas
 (garbanzo beans) in water,
 rinsed and drained
1 tablespoon olive oil
½ teaspoon ground cumin
½ teaspoon chilli powder
½ teaspoon sumac (optional)
½ teaspoon sea salt flakes

For the maftoul salad:
200 g (7 oz/1 cup) maftoul couscous
small bunch (20 g/¾ oz) mint,
 leaves only
large bunch (100 g/3½ oz) flat-leaf
 parsley
6 spring onions (scallions)
½ cucumber, deseeded and finely diced
zest and juice of 1 lemon
2½ tablespoons extra-virgin olive oil
½ teaspoon sea salt flakes

For the pickled radishes:
80 ml (2¾ fl oz) vinegar
2 tablespoons sugar
 (ideally white caster)
½ teaspoon sea salt flakes
200 g (7 oz) radishes, quartered
1 small beetroot (beet) (optional)

For the hummus:
400 g (14 oz) tin chickpeas
 (garbanzo beans) in water,
 rinsed and drained
2½ tablespoons tahini
juice of ½–1 lemon
½ teaspoon sea salt flakes
⅓ garlic clove

flatbreads, to serve (optional)

+ First, preheat the oven to 180°C (350°F/Gas 4). Put the chickpeas in a baking tray and roast for 10 minutes. Remove the tray, stir in the oil, spices and salt then roast for another 10–15 minutes until golden and crisp. Set aside to cool.

+ Meanwhile, bring a medium pan of water to the boil. Add the maftoul and simmer over a medium heat for the time stated on the packet (around 15–18 minutes). Rinse under plenty of cold water then drain.

+ Next, stir together the vinegar, sugar and salt in a small bowl. Add the radishes to the bowl and set aside to lightly pickle.

+ To make the hummus, put the chickpeas in a food processor and blitz with the tahini, juice of half the lemon, salt and garlic until really smooth and silky. Add a few splashes of water to help get the mixture going if it is too dry to blend. Have a taste; you may want to squeeze in more lemon. Set aside.

+ Finely chop the mint leaves, parsley and spring onions (discard any tired-looking outer layers or green tops). Put the herbs, spring onions and cucumber in a large mixing bowl along with the lemon zest and juice, oil and salt. Stir in the drained maftoul, ensuring it's evenly coated in oil and herbs.

——— To assemble

Transfer the hummus, maftoul salad, pickles and crispy chickpeas into nice serving dishes. Take them to the table for everyone to assemble their own plates. If you're really hungry, warm a few flatbreads too.

ROASTED GRAPES, PECANS + WILD ROCKET

with

rosemary croutons

30 MINUTES

SERVES 4

Not only does roasting red grapes intensify their rich, purple tones, it concentrates their natural sugars, making them go sticky and inviting. Teamed with peppery wild rocket, rosemary-baked croutons, toasty, rich pecans and a few naturally seasoning capers, this recipe transforms a fairly standard bunch into something hearty, savoury and pretty extraordinary.

Mighty as it is to eat this salad without any extras, I should highlight that the sweet and sour, almost chutney-like quality that the grapes take on in the oven make it perfect for cutting through charcuterie and oily fish. Tinned sardines or the grilled black pepper mackerel on page 139 make a great pairing.

325 g (11½ oz) seedless red grapes
2½ tablespoons extra-virgin olive oil
2 slices (150 g/5 oz) sourdough bread
3–4 large sprigs (15 g/½ oz) rosemary
1 teaspoon sea salt flakes
100 g (3½ oz) pecan nuts
1 tablespoon capers, drained and roughly chopped
splash of red wine vinegar
150 g (5 oz) wild rocket (arugula)
100 g (3½ oz) baby red gem lettuce
100 g (3½ oz) radishes, finely sliced

+ First, preheat the oven to 200°C (400°F/Gas 6). Lay the grapes in a baking tray, rub with ½ tablespoon of the oil and roast for 18–20 minutes or until lightly caramelised but not yet catching or burning. Transfer the grapes to a plate to cool and pour the tray juices into a small jug or cup.

+ Meanwhile, in a second baking tray, tear the sourdough into small bite-size croutons. Wash and strip the rosemary (discard the woody stalks) then finely chop and stir through the bread along with the salt and remaining oil. Bake for 10 minutes or until golden then transfer to a plate. Add the pecans to the tray and roast for 3 minutes to release their natural oils then set aside.

+ Next, add the capers to the jug containing the reserved grape juice. Stir in the vinegar and set aside. Wash the rocket and gem lettuce in a basin of cold water (this will freshen and crispen the leaves) and pat dry. Shred the gem lettuce lengthwise.

───── To assemble

Place the rocket and gem lettuce on a large platter and scatter the radishes over the leaves. Top with the grapes, croutons and pecans (crushing some in your hands as you scatter). Drizzle over the grape juice dressing to finish and serve immediately while the lettuce is still nice and crisp.

SUBSTITUTES

—

Wild rocket (arugula)
baby kale, large-leaf spinach, watercress

Baby red gem lettuce
cos (romaine) lettuce, frisée

Rosemary
thyme, oregano, dried rosemary

STICKY TOMATO + OLIVE AUBERGINE

with

capers and sultanas

30 MINUTES
SERVES 4

One of those tomato-based dishes that gets even better after a day or two in the fridge; this is my take on a Sicilian *caponata*. The method for this salad is so simple, you can't go wrong. All I would say is it pays to take the time to really brown the aubergines, allowing them to pick up nice colour and go silky soft in the centre.

Smooshed onto some hot toast and topped with lemon-dressed rocket, this is so, so good.

2 firm aubergines (eggplants) (500 g/1 lb 2 oz)
90 ml (3 fl oz) olive oil
1 red onion
2 garlic cloves
2 tablespoons capers, drained
400 g (14 oz) tin chopped tomatoes
30 g (1 oz) sultanas (golden raisins)
1½ tablespoons red wine vinegar
50 g (2 oz) pitted olives (any colour, drained weight)
50 g (2 oz) wild rocket (arugula)
small bunch (20 g/¾ oz) flat-leaf parsley
small bunch (15 g/½ oz) basil
⅓ lemon
4 slices sourdough bread (300 g/10½ oz)

+ First, heat a large frying pan (skillet) over a high heat while you cut the aubergines into large chunks (roughly 2.5 cm/1 in). Add most of the oil to the pan along with the aubergine chunks and cook for 5–6 minutes until golden and beginning to darken on all sides.

+ Meanwhile, peel and halve the onion then slice into thin half-moons. Peel the garlic and slice into thin slivers.

SUBSTITUTES

—

Aubergines (eggplants)
courgettes (zucchini), marrow

Sultanas (golden raisins)
raisins, dried apricots, dried cranberries

Wild rocket (arugula)
watercress, lamb's lettuce

+ Add the remaining oil to the aubergine pan and reduce the heat to low then fry the onion for 3 minutes until beginning to soften. Add the garlic and cook for a further 2 minutes (taking care to not burn the garlic).

+ Add the capers to the pan along with the tomatoes, sultanas, vinegar, olives and a few splashes of water. Increase the heat to high, pop on a lid and cook for 7–10 minutes or until the aubergine is soft in the centre. (Keep an eye on the pan and add a few more splashes of water if it's looking too dry at any point.) Remove from the heat and allow to cool to room temperature. (Place in the fridge if you're making a day or two ahead.)

+ When you're ready to serve, wash the rocket in a basin of cold water (this will freshen and crispen the leaves), pat dry and place in a large mixing bowl. Tear in the herbs (discard the stalks), squeeze over the lemon and gently toss.

——— To assemble

Toast the bread then divide between four plates or a large serving board, as pictured. Smear over the aubergines then top with the lemony rocket.

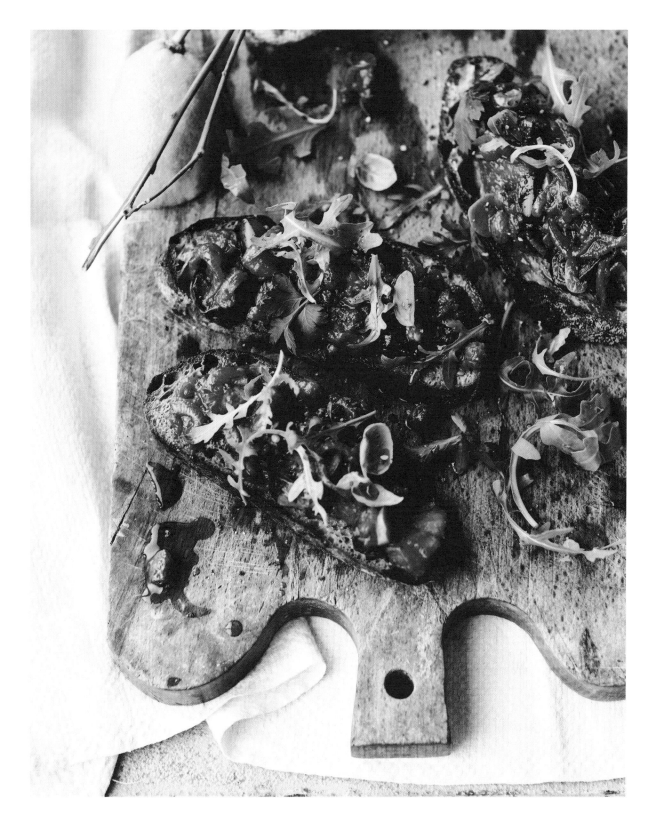

STICKY POMEGRANATE BEETROOT

with

pistachio freekeh
and chickpeas

35 MINUTES

SERVES 4

SUBSTITUTES

—

Freekeh
pearl barley, quinoa, spelt,
brown rice

Pistachios
hazelnuts, pecans, almonds

Flat-leaf parsley
dill, mint leaves

TIP

—

If you don't have pomegranate
molasses, a tablespoon of red wine
or balsamic vinegar mixed with
2½ tablespoons of honey makes
an excellent stand-in.

This is such a great way to celebrate a humble bunch of beetroots; simmering them in small wedges until perfectly tender then coating them in ginger, lemon and syrupy pomegranate until glossy.

I've not included it as a vital step, but if you spot any nice-looking smaller beetroot leaves, it's worth roasting them in a drizzle of oil for a couple of minutes. They take on a crisp-like texture; just amazing scattered over the pistachio-studded freekeh.

Use prepacked pomegranate seeds if deseeding the fruit seems like too much of a faff. Serve with hummus, falafel, kebabs and flatbreads if you're planning on making this the centre of a larger feast.

200 g (7 oz) freekeh or bulgur wheat
1¼–1½ teaspoons sea salt flakes
600 g (1 lb 5 oz) bunch beetroots (beets)
60 g (2 oz) shelled pistachios
large bunch (30 g/1 oz) flat-leaf parsley, finely chopped
2 tablespoons extra-virgin olive oil
1 lemon
400 g (14 oz) tin chickpeas (garbanzo beans) in water, rinsed and drained
30 g (1 oz) fresh ginger, peeled and finely grated
3½ tablespoons pomegranate molasses (see tip)
100 g (3½ oz) prepacked pomegranate seeds or 1 small pomegranate (optional)

+ First, bring a medium pan of water to the boil. Add the freekeh and 1 teaspoon of salt then simmer for the time stated on the packet until tender (around 15 minutes). Rinse under plenty of cold water and set aside to drain completely.

+ Meanwhile, wearing rubber gloves, peel and trim the beetroots then cut into quarter wedges (any smaller ones can be halved). Put in a large pan and cover with water. Bring to the boil then simmer for around 25 minutes or until tender when pierced with a sharp knife. Drain in a colander then return to the pan.

+ While the beetroot is cooking, toast the pistachios in a dry frying pan (skillet) over a high heat for 1–2 minutes to release their natural oils. Transfer to the corner of your chopping board and allow to cool. Put the parsley in a large bowl along with the drained freekeh and half the oil. Slice a cheek/side off the lemon and chop really finely, then add to the bowl along with ¼ teaspoon of salt. Toss the chickpeas through the dressed freekeh then check the seasoning; you may need to add more salt.

+ Add the ginger to the beetroot pan along with the molasses, a squeeze of the lemon and the remaining oil. Heat the pan over a high heat for 1 minute and gently toss to coat the beetroot in the glossy, syrupy juices.

——— To assemble

Transfer the dressed freekeh to a large platter then tip over the beetroot and syrupy juices. If using, scatter over the pomegranate seeds to finish.

GRIDDLED AUBERGINE SUSHI RICE

with

chilled spinach and creamy sesame

35 MINUTES

SERVES 4

SUBSTITUTES

—

Spinach
rainbow chard

Sushi rice
brown rice

Sushi ginger
pickled radish

Edamame
cooked sugar snap peas

TIP

—

To appreciate each element, I find it's best to serve them on nice ceramic dishes then let everyone build their own bowl at the table along with chopsticks and sake, Japanese beer or green tea.

This meal is based on the small-plate accompaniments I like to order at Koya, a Japanese spot in London's Soho where you sit along the open bar with a deep bowl of udon noodles or rice, observing the chefs as they peacefully set about a busy service.

There's charred aubergine, seaweed-inspired chilled spinach, edamame beans, seasoned rice, pickled ginger, shredded spring onion and a creamy umami tahini and sesame dressing.

200 g (7 oz/1 cup) sushi rice
85 g (3 oz) sushi ginger plus
   2 tablespoons pickling juices
125 g (4 oz) frozen podded edamame
   beans
1 large firm aubergine (eggplant)
   (or 8 baby aubergines)
3 tablespoons vegetable oil
1 teaspoon sea salt flakes
250 g (9 oz) spinach
6 spring onions (scallions)

For the dressing:
35 g (1¼ oz) sesame seeds
3½ tablespoons tahini
3½ tablespoons soy sauce
2 tablespoons sugar
   (preferably brown)
1½ tablespoons white wine vinegar

+ First, rinse the rice under cold water in a sieve until the white, milky water turns clear. Next, add the rice and 1½ times the volume of water to a medium pan and cook according to the packet instructions (around 8–12 minutes), then set aside. Once the rice is cold and sticky, spoon over the pickling juices from the ginger (this seasons it beautifully).

+ Next, place the beans in a colander under hot running water for 1 minute, then turn the water to cold and set aside to defrost. Heat a large frying pan (skillet) or griddle pan until smoking. Slice the aubergine into 5 mm (¼ in) lengths. Rub in the oil and cook in a single layer over a high heat for 10–15 minutes or until charred and soft on both sides. (Don't worry about the aubergine picking up colour here as it gives a deep, smoky flavour.)

+ Bring a medium pan of water to the boil and add the salt. Wash the spinach then blanch in the water for 30 seconds. Drain under cold water to prevent further cooking then place in a bowl of very cold water (add ice if you have some).

+ Next, toast the sesame seeds in a small frying pan over a high heat for 1–2 minutes until fragrant and golden. Transfer most of the seeds to a food processor (reserve some for garnish) and blitz with the tahini, soy, sugar and vinegar plus 1–2 tablespoons water until you get a pourable dressing.

+ Shred the spring onions by cutting them finely on an angle (discard any tough green upper layers). Drain the spinach, squeezing out as much excess water as you can.

——— To assemble

You can either divide the rice between four plates and layer up with aubergine, spinach, spring onions, the reserved sesame seeds, beans, ginger and dressing. Or my preferred way: place all the elements in nice individual serving dishes and allow everyone to build their own plate at the table.

ROAST BROCCOLI + CRISPY ONION RICE

with

coconut sambal and pickled radishes

35 MINUTES

SERVES 4

SUBSTITUTES

—

Broccoli
cauliflower, Brussels sprouts

Radishes
deseeded cucumber, mango

Onion
leek, spring onions (scallions)

Most brassicas benefit from being roasted at a high temperature, their edges catching slightly, picking up some of that lovely charred flavour while the inside turns soft and intensely sweet. Here, regular broccoli is the vegetable of choice, but often I'll use cauliflower, slicing it into thick 'steaks'.

Frying onions and garlic until fragrant and crisp takes regular brown rice down a bit of an Indonesian path here, making it a great match for the limey coriander and coconut sambal that cuts so nicely through the meaty broccoli.

2 medium broccoli heads
3 tablespoons vegetable oil
250 g (9 oz/1¼ cups) brown rice
2 limes
½ teaspoon sugar
¼–½ teaspoon sea salt flakes
200 g (7 oz) radishes, finely sliced
1 large onion
2 garlic cloves, peeled and sliced
60 g (2 oz) toasted coconut shavings or desiccated coconut
large bunch (50 g/2 oz) coriander (cilantro)
1–2 green chillies

+   Preheat the oven to 220°C (425°F/Gas 7) then fill a medium pan with water and bring to the boil. Cut the broccoli heads lengthwise into 2 cm (¾ in) thick 'steaks'. Place in a roasting tray in a single layer (spread across two trays if necessary) and drizzle with 1½ tablespoons of the oil. Roast for 25 minutes or until tender and beginning to catch and char at the edges, then set aside.

+   Add the rice to the pan of boiling water and simmer over a high heat for the time stated on the packet (around 20 minutes). Rinse under plenty of cold water to chill it then drain and transfer to a large mixing bowl.

+   Meanwhile, squeeze the juice of 1 lime into a medium bowl. Stir in the sugar and ¼ teaspoon salt. Add the radishes and set aside to quickly pickle.

+   Next, peel and halve the onion then slice into half-moons as finely as you can. Put the remaining oil in a large frying pan (skillet) over a medium heat and fry the onion for 7–8 minutes until golden and beginning to crisp. Add the garlic to the pan and cook for a further 3 minutes over a high heat until the garlic crisps up. Toss the crispy onion and garlic through the rice.

+   Put most of the coconut, most of the coriander and 1 of the chillies into a food processor. Zest in the remaining lime and squeeze in the juice of half. Blitz until you get a rough, textured paste. Check the seasoning; you may want to add more salt, lime juice or chilli.

——————— To assemble

Stir the pickled radishes (not the pickling juice) and reserved coconut through the rice, then pick in the reserved coriander, leaves only. Transfer to a large platter then top with the broccoli. Spoon over the sambal to finish.

CITRUS PRAWN CEVICHE TOSTADAS

with

charred sweetcorn and mashed avocado

35 MINUTES

SERVES 4

While I was writing this book, my friend Ben was exploring in Mexico City. He'd call in every day to see how the testing was going, often remarking on how refreshing and easy ceviche is to make and insisting I include it in my recipes. So here you are, Benny, my version of raw prawns 'cooked' in lime and grapefruit juice; delightful with charred sweetcorn, crispy tortillas, avocado and a cold beer.

Have a go with mixing up the seafood – sea bass, lemon sole and salmon all work brilliantly for ceviche too; just make sure the fish is sustainably caught and super-fresh.

8 small shop-bought corn tortillas (Cool Chile Co. brand is great)
1 tablespoon vegetable oil
160 g (5½ oz) tinned sweetcorn in water (drained weight)
250 g (9 oz) peeled raw king prawns (shrimps)
juice of 3 limes
2 baby shallots or 1 banana shallot, peeled
¾ teaspoon chilli flakes
1 grapefruit
4 radishes, finely sliced
2 avocados, halved and stones removed

+ First, preheat the oven to 180°C (350°F/Gas 4). Divide the tortillas between a few baking trays, brush with the oil then bake for 5–8 minutes, or until golden and crisp. Set aside to cool.

+ Meanwhile, heat a medium frying pan (skillet) until smoking. Rinse the sweetcorn, drain completely then add to the pan (you don't need any oil). Cook for 3–5 minutes or until nicely charred with little black marks. Transfer to a plate to cool.

+ Next, if not already deveined, make a small incision along the back of the prawns and remove the dark black line (the digestive tract). Place the prawns in a medium dish or bowl then squeeze in the limes. Slice the shallots into rounds as finely as you can and add to the bowl along with the chilli flakes. Leave for 7 minutes then turn the prawns over and leave for another 7 minutes. By this point they should be pink and 'cooked'.

+ Next, cut away the top and bottom of the grapefruit, then carefully slice away the peel and white pith. Slice out each segment then finely chop the flesh (discard the membranes). Add to the prawns along with any grapefruit juice. Gently stir in the radishes.

+ Scoop out the avocado flesh and roughly mash with a fork.

——— To assemble

Take the crispy tortillas, ceviche mixture, charred sweetcorn and mashed avocado to the table in nice serving dishes. Allow everyone to build up their own tostadas.

SUBSTITUTES

—

Prawns
sea bass, sea bream, salmon

Radishes
spring onions (scallions)

Corn tortillas
taco shells

TIP

—

You can also shallow-fry the tortillas in a pan of hot vegetable oil until golden. Just be sure to drain on kitchen paper, seasoned with salt.

SHREDDED COCONUT CABBAGE + CHICKEN

with

carrot, lime and coriander

35 MINUTES

SERVES 4

SUBSTITUTES

—

Chicken
turkey, silken tofu

Ginger
lemongrass, kaffir lime leaves

White cabbage
red cabbage, kohlrabi,
mooli (daikon), fennel

Carrots
red/orange (bell) pepper, unripe
mango/papaya

Coconut flakes
desiccated (unsweetened
shredded) coconut,
fresh grated coconut

TIP

—

If you can't find toasted coconut flakes,
just toast the flakes in a medium frying
pan for 2–3 minutes until golden.

If you don't have a julienne peeler, use
a speed peeler to create carrot ribbons
then finely slice lengthwise to create
long, thin strips.

The added joy with this easy recipe is that as you poach the chicken in coconut milk and the aromatics coriander, chilli and turmeric, not only does the meat stay really succulent, but you're left with the most incredible, comforting pan of chicken broth to enjoy alongside your salad. If you fancied, you could even turn it into a noodle soup the next day.

With toasted coconut shavings and coriander leaves being tossed through the lime and coconut milk-dressed veggies, I find the slaw element of this dish is really popular. So another option is to pair it with my ginger roast chicken (page 136).

600 g (1 lb 5 oz) skinless chicken breasts or boneless thighs
400 ml tin coconut milk (full-fat works best)
¾ teaspoon ground turmeric
1½ teaspoons fish sauce
small bunch (20 g/¾ oz) coriander (cilantro)
1 red chilli, roughly chopped
15 g (½ oz) fresh ginger, roughly chopped (no need to peel)
1 garlic clove (optional)
2 carrots
½ white cabbage (400 g/14 oz)
50 g (2 oz) toasted coconut flakes/chips (see tips)

For the dressing:
juice of 2 limes
1½ teaspoons fish sauce

+ First, place the chicken, 350 ml (12 fl oz) of the coconut milk, the turmeric and fish sauce in a medium pan that snugly fits the chicken. Wash the coriander, remove and reserve the leaves and add the stalks to the pan along with the chilli, ginger and garlic. Top up with enough water to just cover the chicken, quickly bring to the boil then reduce to the lowest heat. Poach for 7 minutes then turn the breasts over and cook for a further 7 minutes or until cooked through. Transfer the chicken to a chopping board and allow to cool. Set the pan of cooking broth aside.

+ Meanwhile, top, tail and peel the carrots then, using a julienne peeler (see tips), create long, thin strips and add to a large mixing bowl. Remove any tired-looking outer cabbage leaves then finely shred along with the reserved coriander leaves. Add to the bowl of carrots along with the coconut flakes.

+ Next, make the dressing: stir the remaining 50 ml (2 fl oz) coconut milk, the lime juice and fish sauce together in a small jug or bowl. Toss through the carrot and cabbage mixture, ensuring it's evenly coated in the dressing.

——— To assemble

Place the chicken broth back over a medium heat to warm it through. Transfer the cabbage mixture to a large platter. Then, using two forks, shred the cooled chicken and scatter over the cabbage. Finish by dividing the broth between small bowls or nice vessels then serve immediately.

FIVE-SPICE ROASTED SQUASH + RED RICE

with

toasted cashews and pickled cucumber

40 MINUTES

SERVES 4

A favourite Saturday night treat of mine as a child was crispy duck, pancakes and all the trimmings from our local Chinese takeaway. While the duck was meant to be the centrepiece, it was unpacking the added extras that got me most excited: neat batons of cucumber, finely shredded lengths of spring onion, that small polystyrene container of sticky hoisin sauce.

These days, it's the wonderful variety of pumpkins that arrive in our markets to signify the start of autumn that inspires my cooking more than whole birds, but I still hanker for those nostalgic flavours. So here I rub chunky wedges of squash in those familiar Chinese spices before roasting it until tender and almost caramelised. Along with seasoned red rice, chilli-cucumber pickles, a trusty bottle of hoisin and some cold beers, this has become one of my favourite ways to feast.

Butternut is fine for this recipe, but if you can find it, grab the coquina variety of squash. Most of the big supermarkets stock it these days and for the extra few pence, you'll get way more flavour.

1 large coquina squash
  (around 1 kg/2 lb 3 oz)
1 tablespoon sesame oil
1 tablespoon cumin seeds
1 teaspoon ground cumin
1 tablespoon Chinese five-spice
  powder
1¼ teaspoon sea salt flakes
250 g (9 oz/1¼ cups) red rice
5 spring onions (scallions)

200 g (7 oz) sugar snap peas
3½ tablespoons white wine vinegar
90 g (3 oz) unsalted cashews
2 tablespoons sugar
1 star anise (optional)
½ red chilli, finely sliced
½ large cucumber or 3 baby
  cucumbers
bottle of hoisin sauce (optional)

SUBSTITUTES

—

Coquina squash
butternut squash, pumpkin, sweet potatoes

Red rice
basmati rice, brown rice, wild rice, quinoa

Cashews
peanuts, toasted sesame seeds

TIP

—

Freeze the inner discarded cucumber for popping into gin and tonics.

Taste the rice after 15-20 minutes as I find the cooking time on the packet is sometimes too long.

+ First, preheat the oven to 200°C (400°F/Gas 6). Halve the squash then, using a spoon, scoop out and discard the seeds. Cut into large wedges (don't bother peeling it) then place in a single layer in a large roasting tray. Rub in the oil, spices and 1 teaspoon of salt. Roast for 35–40 minutes or until soft when pierced with a knife and beginning to catch at the edges.

+ Meanwhile, bring a medium pan of water to the boil. Add the rice and cook over a medium heat for the time stated on the packet (around 15–20 minutes). Rinse under cold water, drain completely then transfer to a large bowl. Shred the spring onions and sugar snap peas by cutting them finely on an angle (discard any tough green upper layers of the onions). Stir through the rice along with the remaining salt and ½ tablespoon of the vinegar.

+ While the squash and rice are cooking, toast the cashews in a small frying pan (skillet) over a high heat for 2–3 minutes until golden. Transfer to a small dish to cool. Place the remaining vinegar, the sugar and star anise, if using, in a small bowl and stir in the chilli. Using a speed peeler, create cucumber lengths until you reach the seeds (discard the inner flesh and seeds). Sit the ribbons in the vinegar to lightly pickle.

——— To assemble

Transfer the seasoned rice to a large platter then layer over the squash. Serve with the toasted cashews, cucumber pickle and a bottle of hoisin for the table, if using.

ANCHOVY ROAST PEPPERS

with

smoky tomato beans

For minimal effort, this is a dinner that will transport you to a Mediterranean coastal village. The anchovies do such a beautiful job of seasoning the caramelised pepper juices. With slow-roasted garlic and paprika-tossed butter beans, this dish, washed down with a glass of red, takes you very close to the feeling of being on holiday.

A jar or tin of anchovies is one of my favourite things, especially those that come in retro packaging. But I understand they're an incredibly bold and at times divisive flavour. So if they're not your thing, replace them with crushed olives or capers, ensuring you don't miss out on the incredibly sweet peppers.

40 MINUTES

SERVES 4

2½ tablespoons extra-virgin olive oil
4 red or orange pointed peppers (sadly, green ones don't work for this)
10 anchovies in olive oil
3 garlic cloves, peeled and finely sliced
½ teaspoon chilli flakes
¼ teaspoon freshly ground black pepper
400 g (14 oz) tin butter (lima) beans in water, rinsed and drained
large bunch (30 g/1 oz) flat-leaf parsley, leaves only
6 ripe cherry tomatoes, sliced
juice of ½ lemon
pinch of smoked paprika
4 slices (300 g/10½ oz) sourdough bread (optional)

+   First, preheat the oven to 200°C (400°F/Gas 6) then lightly grease a large roasting tray with ¼ tablespoon of the oil. Slice the peppers in half lengthwise, remove any seeds then place cut side up in the oiled tray. Tear or slice each anchovy in half lengthwise and lay over the peppers. Scatter the garlic over the top and drizzle with ¾ tablespoon of the oil. Sprinkle over the chilli and pepper. Cover with foil (this is important as you don't want the garlic to burn) then roast for 35 minutes. Remove the foil and roast for a further 3–4 minutes. Take out of the oven and allow to cool slightly.

+   Meanwhile, put the butter beans in a large mixing bowl. Finely chop the parsley leaves and add to the beans along with the tomatoes. Squeeze the lemon juice into a small jug or dish along with the remaining oil and the paprika. Stir to combine then pour over the beans. Gently toss to ensure the beans are evenly coated in the dressing.

——— To assemble

Divide the dressed beans between four plates then top each with two pepper halves. Mop up the intensely sweet roasting juices with the bread, if using.

SUBSTITUTES
—

Anchovies
capers, chopped olives

Butter (lima) beans
cannellini beans, chickpeas (garbanzo beans), kidney beans

THYME-ROASTED NECTARINES + SALAMI

with

watercress, salted ricotta and fennel pepper

40 MINUTES

SERVES 4

The stone fruits need a few minutes to caramelise in a hot oven, but really this is a very simple, sunny plate of food, consisting of beautiful, complementary ingredients.

Salted ricotta, or *ricotta salata* as it's sometimes known, is a pressed salted sheep's cheese that I use to naturally season the dish. If you can't find it, other hard, salty cheeses will work nicely too. Please don't be tempted to skip the stage of toasting the fennel seeds; crushed with peppercorns and lemon zest, they add a subtle, aromatic crunch to the leaves.

4 ripe nectarines, halved and stones removed
small bunch (15 g/½ oz) thyme, leaves only
2½ tablespoons extra-virgin olive oil
1½ teaspoons fennel seeds
1½ teaspoons peppercorns
1 lemon
125 g (4 oz) watercress
150 g (5 oz) salami
15 g (½ oz) salted ricotta
4 slices (300 g/10½ oz) sourdough or rye bread

+ First, preheat the oven to 200°C (400°F/Gas 6) and line a roasting tray with baking paper. Place the nectarines cut side up in the tray and scatter over the thyme leaves. Drizzle over 1 tablespoon of the oil then roast for 30 minutes or until soft and beginning to catch and char at the edges. Set aside in the tray to cool slightly.

+ Meanwhile, toast the fennel seeds in a frying pan (skillet) over a high heat for 2–3 minutes to release their natural oils. Transfer to a chopping board then crush and finely chop with the peppercorns. Finely zest over half the lemon then set aside.

+ Next, wash the watercress in a basin of cold water (this will freshen and crispen the leaves), pat dry then add to a large mixing bowl. Drizzle in the remaining oil plus the juice of half the lemon. Use your hands to toss the leaves, ensuring each leaf is nicely coated. Have a taste; you may want to add more lemon juice (keep in mind that the acidity will cut nicely through the rich, sweet fruit).

———— To assemble

Divide the dressed watercress between four plates, place the nectarine halves on top and arrange the salami alongside (it looks nice if you sit the salami in waves rather than flat on the plates). Finely grate or shave over the ricotta then sprinkle over the crushed fennel seed mixture. Spoon any remaining tray juices over the leaves then serve immediately with the bread to mop up the delicious roasting juices.

SUBSTITUTES

—

Nectarines
peaches, apricots, cherries

Salted ricotta
Parmesan, Manchego, pecorino, halloumi, buffalo mozzarella

Watercress
rocket (arugula), pea shoots, dandelion greens

Fennel seeds
cumin seeds, coriander seeds

TIP

—

You can also roast nectarines or peaches like this to make a fantastic dessert. Just switch the oil for a drizzle of honey then spoon over thick natural yoghurt and a scattering of crushed amaretti biscuits. So easy but ridiculously good.

SPRING ROAST VEGETABLE COUSCOUS

with

herby yoghurt and roast lemon

45 MINUTES

SERVES 4

This is a pared-back version of a Sunday roast, but with young, spring vegetables the focus in place of the usual joint of meat. Natural yoghurt is mixed with capers, soft green herbs, cucumber and cider vinegar to form a cool and tangy dressing; a nice seasonal change to hot gravy. Then it's all thrown onto a platter of roast-lemon tossed couscous.

I get overly excited by the different varieties of vegetables that arrive in Britain in the spring, so of course reduce the number of different veg to two or three favourites if that's easier.

300 g (10½ oz) baby or regular beetroots (beets) (a mix of purple and golden varieties is nice if you can get them)
150 g (5 oz) baby or regular carrots
150 g (5 oz) radishes
2 garlic cloves
2 tablespoons olive oil
½ teaspoon sea salt flakes
1 lemon, halved
6 spring onions (scallions)
150 g (5 oz) asparagus
200 g (7 oz) tender-stem broccoli or broccolini
165 g (5¾ oz/1 cup) giant couscous

For the herby yoghurt:
large bunch (20 g/¾ oz) soft green herbs (basil, flat-leaf parsley, tarragon and dill all work well)
1 tablespoon capers, drained and finely chopped
¼ cucumber, deseeded and finely diced
1½ teaspoons cider vinegar
200 g (7 oz) natural yoghurt
½ teaspoon Dijon mustard
sea salt flakes, to taste

SUBSTITUTES

—

Beetroot/carrot
parsnip, turnip

Giant couscous
couscous, spelt, pearl barley, brown rice

Asparagus/broccoli
3 cm (1¼ in) leek chunks, cauliflower

Cider vinegar
red or white wine vinegar, malt vinegar

TIP

—

If you did fancy some meat with this, roasting a chicken with some garlic and thyme (page 136) alongside the veggies is such a stress-free move. Plus any thyme-scented resting juices can be spooned over the couscous.

+ First, preheat the oven to 200°C (400°F/Gas 6) then prepare the vegetables. Scrub the beetroots and carrots under cold running water to remove any dirt or mud. Trim away any tired, tough beetroot stalks; keep any fresh young leaves intact. If using baby beetroot, slice in half lengthwise then place in a large roasting tray. If using regular beetroots, chop into 8 wedges. If using regular carrots, chop into large chunks. If using baby carrots, keep them whole. Add the carrots, radishes and garlic (don't peel it) to the tray then rub in 1 tablespoon of the oil and half the salt. Add the lemon halves to the tray and roast for 15 minutes.

+ Meanwhile, peel any tough outer layers off the spring onions then add to a second baking tray along with the asparagus and broccoli. Rub in the remaining oil and salt then roast for 15 minutes. Give the beetroot tray a shake, remove the garlic, then pop back in the oven for 15 minutes.

+ Once the vegetables are in the oven, bring a medium pan of water to the boil. Add the couscous and boil over a medium heat for the time stated on the packet (around 6–8 minutes). Refresh under cold water, drain, then transfer to a large platter.

+ Next, prepare the yoghurt dressing. Finely chop the herbs and add to a small bowl along with the remaining dressing ingredients. Squeeze in the roasted garlic flesh, then stir and taste; you may want to add some salt.

——— To assemble

Using tongs, squeeze the roasted lemon flesh over the couscous (discard the seeds and skin). Place the vegetables on top then serve with the yoghurt for spooning over.

ROAST BRUSSELS SPROUTS ON BARLEY

with

tahini yoghurt, dates and lemon

45 MINUTES

SERVES 4

SUBSTITUTES

—

Brussels sprouts
broccoli, cauliflower

Hazelnuts
pine nuts, walnuts, almonds

Medjool dates
sour cherries, pomegranate seeds,
dried apricots, dried cranberries

TIP

—

Don't worry if your hazelnuts aren't
blanched. Just rub the nuts between
some sheets of kitchen paper when
they come out of the oven. This will
wipe away most of the papery skins.

Far from any soggy, overboiled territory, this recipe proves that once
roasted, Brussels sprouts can be a thing of beauty. Teamed with herby
pearl barley, sticky Medjool dates, toasted hazelnuts and a rich tahini
yoghurt, they take on a delicious Middle Eastern vibe. This is just
fantastic for tumbling onto a sharing platter or into lunchboxes for
the days ahead.

If you're cooking outside sprout season, broccoli or cauliflower served
in the same manner is just as delightful.

230 g (8 oz) pearl barley
2 bay leaves (optional)
1 lemon, halved
450 g (1 lb) Brussels sprouts
2 tablespoons olive oil
2 teaspoons ground cumin
1 teaspoon ground coriander
1–1½ teaspoons sea salt flakes
35 g (1¼ oz) blanched hazelnuts (see tip)
small bunch (20 g/¾ oz) flat-leaf parsley, leaves only
small bunch (20 g/¾ oz) dill, leaves only
6 Medjool dates, stones removed
½ cucumber, deseeded and finely diced
1 serving tahini lemon yoghurt (page 26)

+ First, preheat the oven to 200°C (400°F/Gas 6) then bring a medium pan of
water to the boil. Carefully add the barley, bay leaves (if using) and one half
of the lemon, then simmer over a medium heat for the time stated on the
packet (around 20–25 minutes). Refresh under plenty of cold water, drain,
then add to a large mixing bowl to cool completely. Remove the bay and
squeeze the lemon flesh over the barley (discard the pips).

+ Meanwhile, trim the Brussels, remove any tired-looking outer leaves,
slice in half then place on a large baking tray in a single layer. Toss in
1 tablespoon of the olive oil, the cumin, coriander and ½ teaspoon of salt.
Roast for 25–30 minutes or until tender and charred at the edges. Add the
hazelnuts to a corner of the baking tray for the last 3–4 minutes of roasting
time to release their natural oils. Remove from the oven and set aside.

+ Finely chop the parsley and dill then stir through the barley along with
½ teaspoon salt, the remaining oil and the juice of the remaining lemon half.
Roughly tear in the dates, add the cucumber then stir to mix. Have a taste;
you may want to add more salt.

——— To assemble

Spread the tahini yoghurt over the base of a large platter. Tumble on the herby
barley then top with the charred Brussels. Bash or crush the hazelnuts then
scatter over to finish.

WARM PUMPKIN PEARL BARLEY

with

roast hazelnuts and crispy sage

45 MINUTES

SERVES 4

Pumpkin and sage are a classic duo, and here they're tossed through chewy pearl barley, roasted hazelnuts and garlicky butter to form a hearty, comforting platter of food.

Roasting the lemon alongside the pumpkin not only makes your kitchen smell fantastic when you open the oven door, but its caramelised flesh adds a surprising citrussy punch to the grains.

1 kg (2 lb 3 oz) pumpkin (sweet varieties like coquina, butternut, onion, kabocha and acorn squash all work well)
1 tablespoon olive oil
¼ teaspoon sea salt flakes
1 lemon
50 g (2 oz) blanched hazelnuts (see tip)
230 g (8 oz) pearl barley
2 bay leaves (optional)
small bunch (15 g/½ oz) chives, finely chopped
1 garlic clove
150 g (5 oz) salted butter
small bunch (20 g/¾ oz) sage, leaves only

+ First, preheat the oven to 200°C (400°F/Gas 6). Halve the pumpkin, scoop out and discard the seeds then cut into chunky wedges (don't bother peeling it). Place in a single layer in a large roasting tray then rub in the oil and salt. Halve the lemon, add to the tray then roast for 35–40 minutes, or until the squash is beginning to char and catch at the edges. Remove from the oven and set aside.

+ Meanwhile place the hazelnuts in a second baking tray and roast for 2–3 minutes to release their natural oils (keep an eye on them as hazelnuts can burn easily). Set aside on a chopping board to cool then roughly crush.

+ Bring a medium pan of water to the boil. Carefully add the barley and bay leaves, if using, then simmer over a medium heat for the time stated on the packet (around 20–25 minutes). Refresh under cold water, drain, then add to a large mixing bowl. Stir in the chives.

+ Peel and crush the garlic then add to a medium frying pan (skillet) along with the butter. Finely chop the sage, keeping some of the smaller leaves whole. Cook the garlic over a low heat for 1 minute until fragrant, and then add in the sage and cook for a further 30–60 seconds until golden and crisp. Toss the sage butter through the barley, reserving a few whole leaves for garnish.

+ Once it's cool enough to handle, squeeze the roasted lemon juice and flesh over the pumpkin.

——— To assemble

Transfer the barley to a large platter and top with the pumpkin wedges. Scatter with the hazelnuts and reserved crispy sage leaves to finish.

SUBSTITUTES

—

Squash
sweet potatoes, cauliflower

Pearl barley
brown rice, spelt, buckwheat

Hazelnuts
walnuts, pecans, almonds

Sage
rosemary, thyme

TIP

—

Don't worry if your hazelnuts aren't blanched. Just rub the nuts between some sheets of kitchen paper when they come out of the oven. This will wipe away most of the papery skins.

ROAST PARSNIPS + CUMIN YOGHURT

with

harissa butter couscous and watercress

In my experience, roast parsnips are one of the first things to disappear from a Christmas dinner table, but they tend to get forgotten about for the rest of their long season. So here parsnips are enjoyed in a new way – with fluffy harissa couscous, handfuls of fresh herbs, crisp greens and a toasted cumin yoghurt.

Remember to pull out the garlic midway through the parsnip roasting time. Once cool enough to handle, you can squeeze its caramelised flesh from the skins, transforming the cumin-infused yoghurt into a dressing that's really rather dreamy.

45 MINUTES

SERVES 4

500 g (1 lb 2 oz) parsnips
2 garlic cloves
1 tablespoon olive oil
¾ teaspoon sea salt flakes
½ tablespoon honey
160 g (5½ oz/1 cup) couscous
30 g (1 oz) butter
2 tablespoons harissa (Belazu rose harissa is great)
1 teaspoon ground cumin
200 g (7 oz) natural yoghurt
60 g (2 oz) watercress
small bunch (20 g/¾ oz) dill, leaves only
small bunch (15 g/½ oz) coriander (cilantro), leaves only

+ First, preheat the oven to 190°C (375°F/Gas 5) then half-fill a kettle. Trim the tops and bases of the parsnips (don't bother peeling them) then slice into rough batons, around 4 x 2 cm (1½ x ¾ in). Place in a roasting tray with the garlic (don't peel it), oil and ¼ teaspoon of salt then roast for 20 minutes. Remove the garlic, give the parsnips a shake then roast for a further 10–15 minutes or until golden. Stir in the honey, roast for a further 2 minutes then set aside to cool.

+ Meanwhile, place the couscous, butter, 1 tablespoon of the harissa and ½ teaspoon salt in a large bowl. Cover with boiling water from the kettle, plus a few extra splashes, then cover and set aside to steam and fluff up.

+ Next, toast the cumin in a small frying pan (skillet) for 30–60 seconds over a high heat until fragrant (take care not to burn it). Transfer to a small bowl and add the yoghurt. Squeeze in the roasted garlic flesh and stir to combine.

+ Wash the watercress in a basin of cold water (this will freshen and crispen the leaves) and pat dry. Finely chop the herbs and, once the couscous has completely cooled, fork them through the grains.

———— To assemble

Transfer the couscous to a large platter. Top with the parsnips and watercress then spoon over the yoghurt. Finish by swirling over the remaining harissa (aim for the oil in the jar more than the paste) then serve immediately.

SUBSTITUTES

—

Parsnips
carrots, pumpkin, swede, turnip

Couscous
farro, spelt, pearl barley

Harissa
tomato paste mixed with chilli paste

Watercress
wild rocket (arugula), lamb's lettuce

MARINATED MUSHROOMS

with

lemon barley and dill cucumbers

45 MINUTES

SERVES 4

Back when I lived by Broadway Market in east London, my Saturday ritual meant picking up lunch early from the *zakuski* stall, before the couple making their popular Middle Eastern/Russian food sold out. This recipe is inspired by them.

Parsley-flecked pearl barley is the substantial grainy base for the marinated mushrooms and dill-yoghurt cucumber here, but if you want to make things even easier, some warm flatbreads would be great for mopping up the garlicky mushroom juices.

The added bonus of this recipe is that everything can be prepared well in advance.

230 g (8 oz) pearl barley
2 bay leaves (optional)
1 lemon, halved
small bunch (15 g/½ oz) flat-leaf
    parsley, leaves only
1½ teaspoon sea salt flakes
1 cucumber
400 g (14 oz) button mushrooms
400 g (14 oz) mixed wild mushrooms

70 ml (2½ fl oz) olive oil, plus
    1 tablespoon (optional)
¼ teaspoon ground cumin,
    lightly toasted
¾ teaspoon ground sumac (optional)
1 small garlic clove
small bunch (15 g/½ oz) dill,
    leaves only
150 g (5 oz) natural yoghurt
1 tablespoon tahini (optional)

+   First, bring a medium pan of water to the boil. Carefully add the barley, bay leaves (if using) and one half of the lemon then simmer over a medium heat for the time stated on the packet (around 20–25 minutes). Refresh under cold water, drain, then add to a large mixing bowl (discard the bay and lemon). Finely chop the parsley then stir through the barley along with ½ teaspoon of salt.

+   Meanwhile, slice the cucumber into rounds as finely as you can (a mandolin is really handy for this) then place in a colander along with 1 teaspoon salt. Set aside to drain (the salt will draw out some of the cucumber's water content).

+   Next, heat a large frying pan (skillet) or griddle pan until smoking. Rub any soil off the mushrooms then slice most of them, keeping some small mushrooms whole. Add to the hot pan and dry-fry for 5 minutes until catching at the edges and turning golden brown. (You're aiming for the mushrooms to cook on dry heat in a single layer, not sweat, so do this stage in a few batches if you're using a small pan.)

+   Stir the oil, cumin and sumac, if using, together in a large mixing bowl. Zest and juice in the remaining lemon half then peel and finely grate or crush in the garlic. Once the mushrooms are cooked, toss through the oil and set aside to quickly marinate.

+   Use your hands to squeeze out any excess water from the cucumber. Finely chop the dill and put in a medium bowl with the cucumber then stir in the yoghurt to combine.

———— To assemble

Divide the barley between four plates. Top with the cucumber yoghurt then the marinated mushrooms. Optional: stir together the tahini and 1 tablespoon of oil in a small jug until smooth then drizzle over the mushrooms to finish.

SUBSTITUTES

—

Pearl barley
spelt, freekeh, brown rice

Dill
mint, chervil

TIP

—

Taste the barley after 20-25 minutes as I find the cooking time on the packet is sometimes too long.

-

3 WAYS WITH…

+

FEAST MENUS

In this chapter I give you simple ideas for injecting new flavour into some old favourites: roast chicken, simply cooked fish, vegetable fritters and perfect eggs. The idea is that you make one of the options then serve it together with a few complementary salads from the previous chapters to form a larger feast.

This is the slower-paced way of cooking and eating with friends and family that I enjoy most on a weekend, when more time's available for roasting a whole marinated bird, opening a bottle of wine, putting on a record and preparing a few easy salads together.

The recipes in this chapter all serve four and are still fairly effortless, so you could easily make them on a busy weeknight with just one of the salads. The vegetable fritters and roast chicken travel particularly well, making them a great lunchbox option for enjoying with any leftover salad the next day. You'll also discover a range of themed menus towards the end of this chapter for times when you want to do a bit more cooking and create a larger, sharing feast.

ROAST CHICKEN
—
3 WAYS

SERVES 4

For succulent meat and crispy skin, I love to roast a whole chicken on a high temperature for a shorter time than is usually suggested; allowing at least 10 minutes of resting before shredding and basting it in the marinade-infused juices before serving.

These cooking times are based on a 1.6 kg (3 lb 8 oz) bird, so adjust the time to the weight of your bird accordingly. You could also use these flavour ideas for marinating chicken breast skewers, thigh or leg pieces if you want to speed things up on a weeknight.

Garlic, Thyme + Spring Onion Roast Chicken

10 spring onions (scallions)
1½ tablespoons olive oil
1 x 1.6 kg (3 lb 8 oz) chicken (removed from the fridge for 15 minutes)
1 lemon, halved
1 small garlic bulb, halved horizontally
small bunch (15 g/½ oz) thyme
1 tablespoon sea salt flakes
½ tablespoon cracked black pepper

+   First, preheat the oven to 200°C (400°F/Gas 6). Wash the spring onions, remove any tired-looking outer layers then place them in a large roasting tray. Rub in ½ tablespoon of the oil then line them up in a double layer to form a little trivet for the chicken to sit on.

+   Slash a few deep incisions into the chicken legs then place the bird on the spring onions. Put the lemon and garlic inside the cavity along with the thyme. Rub the remaining oil all over the skin and inside the cavity then scatter over the salt and pepper. Roast for 65 minutes or until golden and crispy and cooked through. You know the meat is cooked when you insert a skewer or knife into the thigh area and the juices run clear.

+   Allow to rest for at least 10 minutes then squeeze over the roasted lemon and garlic from the cavity. Carve the chicken in the tray, tossing the meat through the sweet spring onions and lemony garlic resting juices before serving.

Ginger, Turmeric + Yoghurt Roast Chicken

The chicken is delicious if you cook it straight away, but if you have time, marinate it in the yoghurt paste for 3–4 hours before roasting and you'll get an even more intense flavour.

3 onions, peeled and halved
1½ tablespoons olive oil
1 x 1.6 kg (3 lb 8 oz) chicken (removed from the fridge for 15 minutes)
1 lemon, halved
50 g (2 oz) fresh ginger, peeled and roughly chopped
150 g (5 oz) natural yoghurt
1 tablespoon ground cumin
1 tablespoon ground coriander
1 tablespoon smoked paprika

½ tablespoon ground turmeric
5 garlic cloves, peeled
1–2 red chillies (depending on how spicy you like it)
1 tablespoon sea salt flakes

+   First, preheat the oven to 200°C (400°F/Gas 6). Rub the onions with ½ tablespoon of the oil, then place them cut side down in the centre of a large roasting tray to form a trivet for the chicken to sit on. Slash a few deep incisions into the legs, pop one lemon half in the cavity, then sit the chicken on the onions.

+   Next, put the ginger in a food processor along with the yoghurt, remaining oil, spices, garlic and chilli. Squeeze in the juice of the remaining lemon half then blitz until you get a smooth paste. Rub the paste all over the chicken including carefully under the breast skin and inside the cavity. Scatter over the salt then roast for around 65 minutes or until golden and crispy and cooked through. You know the meat is cooked when you insert a skewer or knife into the thigh area and the juices run clear.

+   Allow to rest for at least 10 minutes then squeeze over the roasted lemon juices from the cavity. Carve the chicken in the tray, tossing the meat through the spiced resting juices and onions before serving.

Harissa + Coriander Butter Roast Chicken

The chicken is delicious if you cook it straight away, but if you have time, marinate it in the harissa butter for 3–4 hours before roasting, and you'll get an even more intense flavour.

2 leeks
1 x 1.6 kg (3 lb 8 oz) chicken (removed from the fridge for 15 minutes)
1 lemon, halved
70 g (2½ oz) unsalted butter, at room temperature
70 g (2½ oz) harissa paste (Belazu rose harissa is great)
large bunch (30 g/1 oz) coriander (cilantro)
4 garlic cloves, peeled
½ tablespoon sea salt flakes

+   First, preheat the oven to 200°C (400°F/Gas 6). Quarter and wash the leeks (discard the tough upper tops) then place them cut side down in the centre of a large roasting tray to form a trivet for the chicken to sit on. Slash a few deep incisions into the legs, pop one lemon half in the cavity then sit the chicken on the leeks.

+   Next, place the butter, harissa, coriander (leaves and stalks) and garlic in a food processor. Squeeze in the juice of the remaining lemon half then blitz until you get a smooth paste. Rub the paste all over the chicken including carefully under the breast skin and inside the cavity. Scatter over the salt then roast for around 65 minutes, or until golden and crispy and cooked through. You know the meat is cooked when you insert a skewer or knife into the thigh area and the juices run clear.

+   Allow to rest for at least 10 minutes then squeeze over the roasted lemon juices from the cavity. Carve the chicken in the tray, tossing the meat through the resting juices and sweet leeks before serving.

SIMPLY
COOKED
FISH
—
3 WAYS

SERVES 4

I'm aware that people are often a bit scared of cooking fish, so these are a few effortless methods with simple flavours added to make something special. A fishmonger will do any gutting, cleaning and filleting for you. So it's just a case of adding a few herbs, slices of citrus and seasoning to the prepared fish then popping it in a hot oven or under the grill.

Roast Lemon, Dill + Spring Onion Trout

4 x small, whole trout, gutted and cleaned
2 tablespoons olive oil
2 lemons
8 spring onions (scallions)
small bunch (30 g/1 oz) dill
1 teaspoon sea salt flakes

+ First, preheat the oven to 200°C (400°F/Gas 6) then rub ½ tablespoon of the oil over a roasting tray. Next, slice the lemon into 5 mm (¼ in) rounds. Wash the spring onions, remove any tired-looking outer layers and trim away 2 cm (¾ in) from the green tops. Divide the lemon slices, spring onions and dill between the fish cavities. Rub over the remaining oil then scatter with the salt. Roast for 20 minutes or until the skin is crisp and the flesh is soft to touch.

Steamed Ginger, Lime + Lemongrass Sea Bass

Lightly steaming fish in baking paper is a super-easy way to ensure it stays really soft and delicate; just make sure the parcel is well sealed.

4 x 100 g (3½ oz) sea bass fillets
30 g (1 oz) fresh ginger
2 limes
2 lemongrass stalks
small bunch (20 g/¾ oz) coriander (cilantro)

+ First, preheat the oven to 200°C (400°F/Gas 6). Slice the ginger and limes, halve the lemongrass stalks lengthwise and wash the coriander (leaves and stalks). Cut 4 sheets of baking paper to roughly 30 x 30 cm (12 x 12 in).

+ Place a quarter of the ginger and lime slices on the end of one sheet, top with a sea bass fillet, half a lemongrass stalk and a quarter of the coriander. Splash over a tablespoon of water then fold in the left- and right-hand sides. Roll up the remaining paper (keeping the sides tucked in) to make a parcel, then fold the end to seal it and place on a baking tray, seal side down. (If you wanted to be extra secure, you could also make a second parcel with tin foil.) Repeat with the remaining fillets then bake for 12–15 minutes.

2 lemons
4 small whole mackerel, gutted and cleaned
2 tablespoons olive oil
1 teaspoon sea salt flakes
2 teaspoons cracked black peppercorns

+   First, preheat a grill (broiler) to high. Next, cut the lemons into 5 mm (¼ in) slices. Place the mackerel on a baking tray (check it fits under the grill) then make six shallow slashes on the side of each fish. Stuff with the lemons then rub in the oil. Flake the salt and pepper over and inside the cavities then grill for 5 minutes. Flip the fish over then grill for another 5 minutes, or until the skin is crispy and charred and the flesh is soft to the touch.

VEGETABLE FRITTERS

—

3 WAYS

SERVES 4

The key to brilliant fritter-making is a touch of bravery when frying them off. Test that your oil is hot and bubbling with a pinch of mixture then allow the fritters a few minutes on one side before moving them about in the pan too much. This will keep them intact, allowing them to develop a golden, crispy exterior.

In the worst-case scenario, any broken fritters can just be squidged back together; you can't go wrong.

If you're trying to get ahead, you can either shape and refrigerate the fritters, then fry them just before eating. Or cook the whole batch and reheat them in a moderate oven for a few minutes. They're delightful at room temperature too.

Courgette, Halloumi + Potato Fritters (makes 8)

2 courgettes (zucchini) (300 g/10½ oz)
1 large potato (250 g/9 oz)
225 g (8 oz) halloumi
small bunch (20 g/¾ oz) dill
2 eggs
150 ml (5 fl oz) rapeseed or vegetable oil
1 lemon, cut into wedges

+   First, using the large side of a box grater, grate the courgettes and potato (including the skin). Grab handfuls of the grated vegetables and squeeze out any water then place in a large sieve or colander. Set aside in the sink to further drain for 10 minutes. (It's important to try to remove as much water as possible because then you'll get lovely crisp fritters that stay intact while frying.)

+   Meanwhile, drain the halloumi then grate into a large mixing bowl. Finely chop the dill (leaves and stalks) then add to the bowl. Crack in the eggs and whisk with a fork in one side of the bowl. Stir in the drained vegetables then shape into 8 fritters.

+   Next, put the oil in a large frying pan (skillet) over a medium–high heat and line a few plates with kitchen paper. After a few minutes, test the oil is hot enough by adding a pinch of the fritter mixture to the pan. If it sizzles and bubbles, you're ready for frying. Gently place the fritters in the pan (lay them away from you) and cook for 3–4 minutes on each side until golden and crisp. Using a slotted spoon or fish slice, transfer the fritters to the lined plates, allowing the kitchen paper to soak up any excess oil. Serve with the lemon wedges.

280 g (10 oz) tinned sweetcorn (drained weight)
1 lime
6 spring onions (scallions)
1–2 red chillies (depending on how spicy you like them)
3 tablespoons plain (all-purpose) flour
2 eggs
150 ml (5 fl oz) vegetable or rapeseed oil
¼ teaspoon sea salt flakes

+   First, drain the sweetcorn in a colander then place in a large mixing bowl. Zest the lime, finely shred the spring onions and chillies and add them to the bowl along with the flour. Crack in the eggs then whisk with a fork in one side of the bowl. Stir to combine the mixture then shape into 8 fritters.

+   Next, put the oil in a large frying pan (skillet) over a medium–high heat and line a few plates with kitchen paper. After a few minutes, test the oil is hot enough by adding a pinch of the fritter mixture to the pan. If it sizzles and bubbles, you're ready for frying. Gently place the fritters in the pan (lay them away from you) and cook for 3–4 minutes on each side until golden and crisp. Using a slotted spoon or fish slice, transfer the fritters to the lined plates, allowing the kitchen paper to soak up any excess oil. Sprinkle over the salt, cut the lime into wedges and serve.

Sweet Potato + Coriander Fritters (makes 16 small)

3 large sweet potatoes (800 g/1 lb 12 oz)
large bunch (30 g/1 oz) coriander (cilantro)
2½ teaspoons soy sauce
90 g (3 oz/¾ cup) plain (all-purpose) flour
1½ teaspoons sea salt flakes
40 g (1½ oz) butter
1 tablespoon olive oil
1 lemon, quartered

+   First, bring a large pan of water to the boil. Next, peel and roughly chop the sweet potatoes then carefully place in the pan and simmer for 20 minutes or until soft. Drain thoroughly in a colander and allow to steam for 2 minutes.

+   Meanwhile, wash the coriander under cold water and pat dry. Finely chop the stalks and roughly chop the leaves then add to a large mixing bowl along with the soy, flour and salt. Add the potatoes then, using a fork, mash until the mixture is combined.

+   Next, put half the butter and half the oil in a large frying pan (skillet) over a medium heat. Line two plates with kitchen paper. Dollop heaped tablespoons of the potato mixture into the pan and cook for 5 minutes on one side until golden and crisp. Flip and cook the other side for a further 5 minutes then transfer to the kitchen paper to absorb any excess oil. When you've cooked half the mixture, add the remaining butter and oil to the pan and repeat with the remaining mixture. Serve with the lemon wedges to squeeze over.

ABOVE AND RIGHT:

Courgette, Halloumi
+ Potato Fritters (page 140)

Sweetcorn, Lime + Chilli Fritters (page 141)

PERFECT
EGGS
—
3 WAYS

Sometimes all that's needed to complete a simple meal is a nicely cooked egg. These are my tried and tested methods for the perfect, oozy yolk-to-cooked-white ratio. Chilli is added to the frying method, and steaming them in a spiced-tomato sauce gives you a rich shakshuka.

Boiled Eggs

+ Fill a medium pan with water and bring to the boil. Carefully add the eggs then simmer over a medium heat for 6 minutes. Remove with a slotted spoon and plunge into a bowl of cold water to stop them cooking any further. If you gently crack the base of the eggs just before you add to the cold water, they will be easier to peel.

+ For hard-boiled: follow the steps above but simmer for 9 minutes.

Chilli Fried Eggs

1 red chilli
3 tablespoons vegetable oil
4 eggs

+ Finely chop the chilli (I leave the seeds in but remove them if you don't want your eggs too spicy). Put the oil in a large non-stick frying pan (skillet) over a medium heat then crack in the eggs. Scatter the chopped chilli over the whites then cook for 2–3 minutes, or until the white is firm and crispy at the edges and the yolks golden and oozy. As they're frying, carefully spoon any excess oil over the whites to help fry the chilli.

Shakshuka

small bunch (20 g/¾ oz) parsley
2 tablespoons olive oil
1 medium onion, peeled and finely chopped
2 garlic cloves, peeled and finely chopped
½ teaspoon sea salt flakes
½ teaspoon sugar
½ tablespoon ground cumin
1 tablespoon paprika
2 x 400 g (14 oz) tins tomatoes
4 eggs

+ Wash then finely chop the parsley stalks (reserve the leaves). Put the oil in a large, deep frying pan (skillet) over a medium heat and fry the parsley stalks and onion for 6–8 minutes until soft. Add the garlic, salt, sugar and spices, cook for 1–2 minutes then add the tomatoes then reduce the heat to low and simmer for 6 minutes, stirring occasionally.

+ Next, make four divots in the sauce and break in the eggs. Cover with a lid and cook for 4–6 minutes or until the eggs are just set. Roughly chop the parsley leaves, scatter over then serve immediately.

TIP
—

You can make the tomato sauce ahead of time then just reheat and crack in the eggs when you're ready to eat.

Have a play with the herbs and spices too; harissa, dill and feta are all nice scattered over at the end.

Seasonal Feasts

SUMMER
—

**Grilled Black Pepper +
Lemon Mackerel**

139

**Charred Prawns,
Cannellini Beans + Fennel**
with salsa verde and sourdough

46

Pickled Watermelon + Halloumi Spelt
with sundried tomatoes, sugar snap peas and mint

66

AUTUMN
—

**Garlic, Thyme + Spring Onion
Roast Chicken *or* Courgette,
Halloumi + Potato Fritters**

136 + 140

Warm Pumpkin Pearl Barley
with roast hazelnuts and crispy sage

130

**Braised Olive +
Puy Lentil Casarece**
with garlic, lemon and radicchio

78

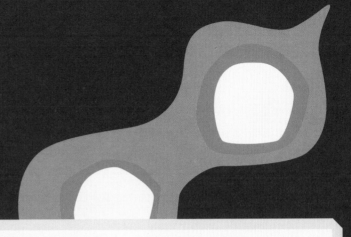

WINTER
—

**Garlic, Thyme + Spring Onion
Roast Chicken**

136

Orange Carrot Freekeh
with cranberries and walnuts

90

Radicchio, Stilton + Pear
with toasted walnuts and rye croutons

32

Regional Feasts

INDIAN
–

**Ginger, Turmeric +
Yoghurt Roast Chicken**

136

**Roast Broccoli +
Crispy Onion Rice**
with coconut sambal and pickled radishes

117

**Pickled Red Cabbage,
Ginger + Pomegranate Slaw**
with cumin, lime and coriander

44

MIDDLE EASTERN
—

**Harissa + Coriander Butter Roast Chicken *or*
Courgette, Halloumi + Potato Fritters**

137 + 140

Crispy Chickpeas + Parsley Maftoul Couscous
with hummus and pickles

109

Sticky Pomegranate Beetroot
with pistachio freekeh and chickpeas

115

SOUTH EAST ASIAN
—

Sweetcorn, Lime + Chilli Fritters

141

Steamed Ginger, Lime + Lemongrass Sea Bass

138

Shredded Mango, Lime + Peanuts
with tomatoes and chilli

107

Brunch Feast

THANK YOU

At the end of 2015, I tearily packed up my desk at Jamie Oliver's Nile Street office and said farewell to some of the most dedicated, talented people in food. It was terrifying. I'd stepped away from a secure, rewarding marketing job, learning directly from my heroes. But niggling away at me was the desire for challenge outside of my desk-based comfort zone, to be hands-on with food. This cookbook is quite simply the culmination of all the brilliant, generous people I've been so very lucky to learn from and feast with these past few years on my freelance cooking adventure.

Philip. 12 years of putting up with me banging on about food every waking minute deserves recognition. For the late-night supermarket dashes and endless rounds of washing up, I can't thank you enough.

Claire and Den. Pure happiness is Friday night at Sunnybank; spag bol, red wine, the retelling of stories we've heard a million times over. Thank you for introducing me to food culture from a young age. Mum, thanks for making the kitchen table the centre of our lives. Dad, thanks for taking me to school on your motorbike, for wearing fedora hats and neon cycling tops, and for instilling the value of just being yourself; I'm a stronger character for all of it.

Kate and Stu. I've felt you both cheering me on from the sidelines at every stage of creating this book; it's a wonderful feeling, thank you.

Ben and Tim. Ben, how you managed to pull off being in my kitchen every day, chatting and guiding me through the recipe development whilst also travelling the world is an absolute wonder. Your commitment to our friendship from the other hemisphere is everything; a huge amount of this book comes from you. Tim, thank you for the recipe testing and for welcoming me with open arms into Australia.

Rosie. This book wouldn't be here without you giving me a good sitting down and talking to. Not cooking alongside you every day is a sad thought, but you're always guiding me as I ask myself 'What would Rosie do?'. Thanks for everything, queen.

Jono. I'm in constant awe of your talent and generosity. Thank you for pulling me aside on that farm weekend and nagging me to write this book; I hope I've done you proud.

Linzi. I'm sorry I didn't include your raspberry and mushroom stir-fry as a recipe, but I'm saving it for the cover of book number two! Seriously, though, for letting me encroach any form of personal space, for the laughter, costumes and everything in between, I adore you.

Matt. I could spend all day sinking into your photography, and I'm still pinching myself that I got to work with you on this. Thank you for bringing my food to life. But more than that, for the best disco playlists, for entertaining us with your funny stories, and for going way above and beyond. That shoot week last October was a truly magical one thanks to you. I'll always miss and treasure it.

Kajal. Wow! You let me make a cookbook, something I'd only ever dreamed about. Thank you for taking a chance on little, unknown me, for listening to my vision from day one and for pulling together the most incredible team.

Abby. From France to Elm House and all the lunch dates in between, what a special year we've had together. Thank you for making the early starts and late finishes on shoot days seem so effortless, for always smiling, and for cooking up a storm in your peaceful, beautiful way.

Evi. Just looking at your designs makes me do a happy dance. Thank you so, so much for bringing the whole concept alive.

Claudia L. You charred that mackerel to perfection and it's one of my favourite shots in the book – thank you!!! I can't wait for your chef residency at *Elliott*'s and to see where your talent takes you next...

Linda. Your sourcing was perfection, it's as simple as that. Thank you.

Jenny and Neil. For the thorough recipe testing, proofreading and ongoing support for Philip and I, thank you. I'm excited to spend more time eating and walking with you both back in Scotland.

Hamish. It's your love of making simple salads to enjoy with good wine on the rooftop with us all that inspired this book, so thanks.

Sarah and Sam. Thanks for letting me play in your beautiful home. Sarah, it was you that introduced me to the creative side of food and to the joy of having colour charts on hand at all times. Thank you for pushing me at Jamie's, for instilling high, thorough standards and for linking me up with Jacque and co. I owe you.

Jackie. None of this would have been possible if it wasn't for you taking me in and setting me up. Not once but twice. Fairy godmother doesn't even begin to cover it.

Jacque. My cooking adventure began with you at Cornersmith. Thank you for all the laughs. So many laughs!

Thank you also to those that have encouraged and inspired me (even if blissfully unaware): Jade Bajai, Aya Nishimura, Susie Theodorou, Sophie Dickins, Kerri Palmer, Tony Stone, Jamie Oliver, Aimi Duong, Natalya Watson, Emily Hurdiss, Craig Goodare, Tiffany Crouch, Pete Begg, Georgina Hayden, Louise and Colin Elliott, Sam Harris, Steph Howard, Becca Jones, Claudia Gschwend, Rebecca Coats, Léa Deroubaix, Kathrin-Nina Späth.

Plus a huge thank you to the makers and artists that loaned me your beautiful work: Ren London, Grain & Knot, Hampson Woods.

Thank You.

JESSICA ELLIOTT DENNISON

Jess is a cook and stylist based between London and Edinburgh. She's self-taught in the kitchen, her flavours and straightforward approach inspired by seasonal vegetables and time spent living in Sydney and Bangkok.

Previous to cooking for books, magazines and TV, Jess worked in marketing as part of Jamie Oliver's retail team, responsible for the chef's 1,000-product food and homeware range. It was there that she became friends with photographer and director Matt Russell.

Jess's newest project is *Elliott's*; a neighbourhood cafe, workshop and supperclub space tucked behind Edinburgh's leafy meadows. There she prepares a simple weekly-changing menu, led by the seasons and Scotland's best produce.

INDEX

Published in 2018 by Hardie Grant Books, an imprint of Hardie Grant Publishing

Hardie Grant Books (London)
5th & 6th Floors
52–54 Southwark Street
London SE1 1UN

Hardie Grant Books (Melbourne)
Building 1, 658 Church Street
Richmond, Victoria 3121

hardiegrantbooks.com

British Library Cataloguing-in-Publication Data. A catalogue record for this book is available from the British Library.

Salad Feasts by Jessica Elliott Dennison

ISBN: 978-1-78488-164-1

Publisher: Kate Pollard
Commissioning Editor: Kajal Mistry
Publishing Assistant: Eila Purvis
Art Direction: Evi O. / Evi O. Studio
Photographer: Matt Russell
Photography Assistants: Sam Harris, Becca Jones, Steph Howard and Claudia Gshwend
Food Stylist: Jessica Elliott Dennison
Food Stylist Assistant: Abby Camilleri
Prop Sourcing: Linda Berlin and Ginger Whisk
Editor: Lorraine Jerram
Proofreader: Sarah Herman
Indexer: Cathy Heath

Colour Reproduction by p2d
Printed and bound in China at Toppan Leefung, DongGuan City, China